simply
BUSINESS

B1

ANGELA LLOYD

EFFECTIVE ENGLISH FOR DOING YOUR JOB

D1619642

This book is also available online on

www.scook.de/eb

Please accept the terms and conditions to use the eBook.

Book Code: j7m6u-kzp5y

Cornelsen

Welcome to Simply Business B1

Who is the book for?

Simply Business is a learner-based course with a hands-on focus, designed to meet the needs of in-work learners who want to use English effectively. The course features real people and companies and uses authentic materials from their day-to-day work.

Reflecting global trends, the course helps you develop awareness and sensitivity towards different accents, varieties of English and cultural differences in communication style.

Simply Business offers plenty of opportunity to apply what you learn to your own work context. Many personalized exercises encourage you to use and adapt the language learned to perform the tasks you have to do on a daily basis. In addition to the functional language, talking points and group projects give you the chance to develop fluency by discussing and presenting workplace-related issues.

How is the book structured?

Simply Business consists of eight units which focus on everyday business communication, working internationally, global English and cultural issues, featuring information and recordings with business people from around the world.

Each unit contains:

● an introduction to the unit topic to get you talking

● topic-related language work using authentic examples of emails, telephone calls, and workplace interaction provided by real business people

● **Language Focus** (1) in which useful grammar or language structures can be practised in context

● **info boxes** (2) and **company boxes** (3) which focus on the situation in your company

● **files** with additional background information and partner exercises

● a **Global English** page, featuring a range of English speakers and focusing on areas that can cause communication breakdown.

● an **Over to you** page (4) including a **project** (5) where you can apply what you have learned

● a **Progress check** page with an outlook on the next unit

● For easy orientation, each page has a footer (6) which identifies the topic of that page.

● The **appendix** includes video worksheets, (partner) files and an answer key to the Progress check pages.

What additional features does the course offer?

In addition to the printed material, **Simply Business** includes

- **four films** which you can watch using the DVD or the PagePlayer app. The films can be watched during or outside class, but are all directly connected to the unit content.

In three of the films you see other non-native speakers performing the kind of tasks you may have to do at work. These unscripted films feature non-native speakers of English, whose English may not always be perfect, but who communicate their messages effectively to an international audience. The fourth film focuses on varieties of English and gives information about various business cultures.

- **PagePlayer app.** In addition to the accompanying CD and DVD, you can also listen to all audio tracks and watch the films on your smartphone or tablet using the PagePlayer app.

You need to download the Page-Player app by scanning the QR code on the right. Once you have the app, anytime you see an audio or film icon in the book, you can scan the page and will be able to listen or watch the appropriate file.

- **Vocabulary app.**
With this app you can test your knowledge of the B1-level vocabulary which appears in Simply Business. The app uses a flashcard system for learning and practising words and phrases. To download the app, scan the QR code on the right.
www.cornelsen.de/vokabeltrainer

- **Word lists** and **additional language practice** online:
www.cornelsen.de/simply

We hope you enjoy learning English with Simply Business!

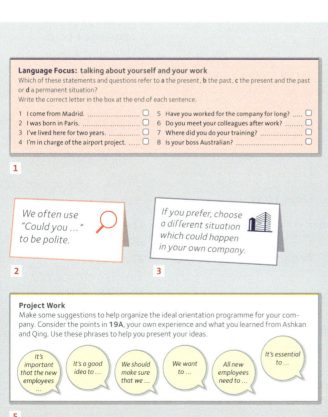

01

Starting anew

02

Describing your company

03

Speaking informally

04

Choosing a location

Appendix

01 Starting anew

1

A Discuss possible connections between these pictures and the first day in a new job.

B **02))** Now listen to what a career consultant says. What other topics does he mention?

2

A Listen again and fill in the missing words.

1 Do _____ to make a good impression.

2 Make _____ you arrive at work on time.

3 It's a _____ to test the route during rush hour.

4 You have a lot to learn about your new job and your new company so don't _____ ask questions.

5 You can _____ you'll impress everyone by knowing the latest company news.

6 If you don't know where people eat lunch, it's _____ to take some sandwiches with you.

B What help and advice would you give to someone on their first day? Present your own golden rules using some of the phrases you completed in **A**.

It's a good idea to … *Don't be afraid to …* *It's essential to …* *Make sure you …*

3

Make your own sentences using expressions from the tables.

make/ create	a good/ bad/strong	impression	by	-ing
			on	(someone)
a way to / you can	impress	(someone)	is by	-ing
			by	

See how the career consultant uses these expressions by looking at the transcript on page 80.

4

A 👥 Work with a partner to complete three short dialogues.

Partner A → **File 1**, page **70**. **Partner B** → **File 2**, page **72**.

B All three conversations take place on the first day in a new job. Who are the two people speaking in each one and what is the specific situation?

5

A Match the two parts of each introduction. Which are more formal?

1 Good morning. May
2 Have you
3 Hello, my name's
4 I'd like to

A met Andy?
B Tina.
C I introduce myself?
D introduce you to my new colleague.

> *First names or family names?*
> *What's the norm in your company?*
>
> *family name = last name = surname*

B Imagine it's your first day in a new job. How would you introduce yourself?

You are speaking to ...	your new boss	a colleague	a group of co-workers
greeting			
introduction			
new position			
I'm looking forward to ...			

6

A Imagine these embarrassing situations. What might each person say?

Situation 1
You are having a conversation with a new employee on their first day in the company. A co-worker you don't know very well comes over to join the conversation. You can't remember the name of either of them.

Situation 2
You are working at your desk when your boss comes into your office with a new co-worker. She introduces you but says your name incorrectly. You know that your name is not easy!

Situation 3
A new colleague has just introduced himself to you and told you something about his background. He has a very strong accent and you didn't understand what he said.

B Can you think of any other situations like these?

C 👥 Now role-play one of the situations.

7 **03)))** When you introduce yourself to a new member of staff, you often describe your responsibilities. Complete the statements with the correct prepositions, then listen to check your answers.

1 We're responsible _____ developing innovative new products.

2 Most of the suppliers we deal _____ are in Asia.

3 I'm in charge _____ the transportation of goods to our customers.

4 I'm familiar _____ international accounting standards.

5 Our department focuses _____ controlling the quality of our products.

6 I have a lot of experience _____ organizing orientation programmes for new staff.

---

8 **A 04)))** Look at the organogram and listen to five colleagues describing their responsibilities. Match them to the departments they work in.

> Make an organogram of your own company. Use your company intranet to check the information.

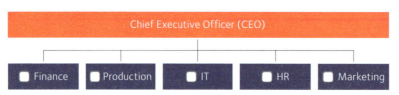

Chief Executive Officer (CEO)

| ☐ Finance | ☐ Production | ☐ IT | ☐ HR | ☐ Marketing |

B Make a list of the departments in your company. Use expressions in **7** and the words below to help you explain what each department does.

arranges • buys • checks • creates • develops • looks for • maintains • organizes • sells

---

9 **Language Focus: talking about yourself and your work**
Which of these statements and questions refer to **a** the present, **b** the past, **c** the present and the past or **d** a permanent situation?
Write the correct letter in the box at the end of each sentence.

1 I come from Madrid. .... ☐
2 I was born in Paris. .... ☐
3 I've lived here for two years. .... ☐
4 I'm in charge of the airport project. ..... ☐

5 Have you worked for the company for long? ..... ☐
6 Do you meet your colleagues after work? .... ☐
7 Where did you do your training? .... ☐
8 Is your boss Australian? .... ☐

---

10 Choose the expressions that complete the sentences correctly.

1 We built our first factory in India ... .
   a ☐ for three years   b ☐ three years ago

2 Our team has a meeting ... .
   a ☐ last week   b ☐ every Monday morning

3 Sam's my colleague. He's worked here ... .
   a ☐ for a month   b ☐ a month ago

4 She was my boss ... I worked for ITC.
   a ☐ since   b ☐ as   c ☐ when

5 I've changed departments three times ... .
   a ☐ since I started   b ☐ when I started

6 Our colleagues from India visited us ... .
   a ☐ every month   b ☐ last month

11

A What else would you tell a new employee about your history with the company?

Take a sheet of paper and write one sentence to introduce yourself. Now pass the pieces of paper around so that everyone can write one question for each other person in the group.

Where did you work before you came here?

I've worked here for five years.

What does your department deal with?

What are you in charge of?

Have you always worked in this field?

B Decide what information you would want to give about yourself to a new member of staff, using the questions to help you. Now pair up and take turns to introduce yourselves. Ask further questions if you like. What information is appropriate to give in this situation?

12

A Make notes on what you would like to know about a new co-worker.

B What questions could you ask to find out the information?

Personal information

New position

Previous experience/ training

13

A Read part of a blog written by Monika from Pune, India, about breaking the ice with new colleagues. How suitable is this information for your company? What tips would you give?

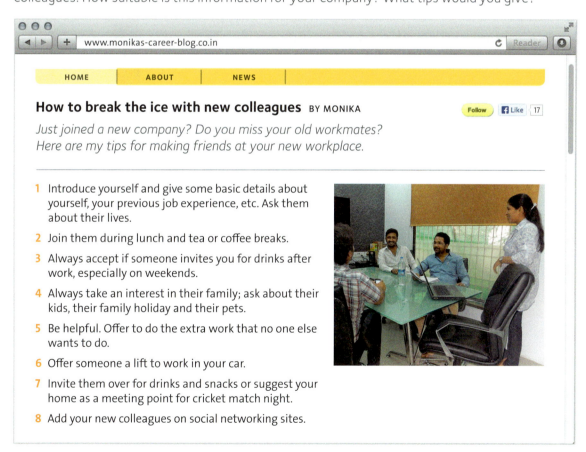

www.monikas-career-blog.co.in

| HOME | ABOUT | NEWS |

How to break the ice with new colleagues BY MONIKA

Follow · Like 17

Just joined a new company? Do you miss your old workmates?
Here are my tips for making friends at your new workplace.

1 Introduce yourself and give some basic details about yourself, your previous job experience, etc. Ask them about their lives.
2 Join them during lunch and tea or coffee breaks.
3 Always accept if someone invites you for drinks after work, especially on weekends.
4 Always take an interest in their family; ask about their kids, their family holiday and their pets.
5 Be helpful. Offer to do the extra work that no one else wants to do.
6 Offer someone a lift to work in your car.
7 Invite them over for drinks and snacks or suggest your home as a meeting point for cricket match night.
8 Add your new colleagues on social networking sites.

B 05)) Monika's blog gives tips for making friends at work. Now listen to her speaking to her colleagues and decide which tip each offer or question refers to.

14

A The lunch hour is a good time to get to know your colleagues better. Read about workplace lunch routines around the world. How would you prefer to spend your lunch break? Why?

We don't have a canteen and our office is in an expensive part of town so most of us usually bring food from home and eat in our break room. There are fridges, microwaves and a television in there. We take around one hour. In the summer we tend to eat salads but in the winter we prefer meat stew. On sunny days we go for lunch outside in a park and then have a walk along the river. On the first Friday of the month we go out for lunch to the carritos. Then we take a longer break and work later if we're very busy. Carritos are snack bars located along the coast and they sell the best steaks in Argentina!

Carolina works for an IT company in Buenos Aires, Argentina

Our lunch break is about one-and-a-half hours, usually from 12 o'clock. We go to a restaurant nearby for a simple meal

like noodles or rice with vegetables or meat. We don't have a company canteen. It's not worth it because restaurants are so cheap. After lunch we go back to the office for a nap. Sometimes we have a longer lunch with lots of dishes, for example if we have a guest or if the weekend is coming up. I enjoy this because people have a joke, and we have some interesting conversations. In China, people don't take food from home for their lunch.

Yang works for a German engineering company in Shanghai, China

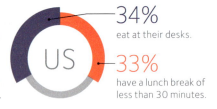

UK — **20%** take a full hour for lunch.

14% hope to impress the boss by taking a shorter break.

US — **34%** eat at their desks.

33% have a lunch break of less than 30 minutes.

We share a canteen with the other companies in our office complex. Officially our lunch break is 30 minutes but in fact it depends on how busy we are. Sometimes we finish in 15 minutes, but if we have time, we have what you could call a working lunch and that may take up to an hour. The food in the canteen is good and not expensive so most people eat there every day. There's a choice of two dishes with meat or fish, and one vegetarian option, plus desserts, of course. Here you can see Pekka and me enjoying our lunch with a glass of home-made beer. It's non-alcoholic, by the way! I think everyone finishes their lunch with at least one big cup of coffee.

Arto works for a technical consultancy in Varkaus, Finland

B Which of these questions do all three employees answer?

1 ☐ How long is your lunch break?
2 ☐ How much do you usually pay for your lunch?
3 ☐ Does your company have its own canteen?
4 ☐ Is there a company rule that you must take a lunch break?
5 ☐ Do you have time to socialize with colleagues during your lunch break?
6 ☐ Do you bring a packed lunch from home?

15

👥 Think about how you and your colleagues spend your lunch break and make some notes based on the questions in **14B**. Now discuss your own routine in a small group using the words and expressions on this page to help you.

Our lunch break …   As far as I know, …   We tend to …   I usually …   Most of us …

16   **A** Understanding accents can be difficult. How well do you understand regional accents in your country? Discuss with a partner.

B   **06**))) You are going to hear the same short text spoken by people from different countries. Write the text as you listen. After listening to all the speakers, compare the text with a partner.

C   Can you guess the native language of each speaker? Was one of the speakers very difficult/ not very difficult to understand? Why do you think this was?

---

17   Now read an online forum about problems with accents. Are any of the ideas new to you? Which tips would you use?

> Remember the phrases you used to talk about the first day at work.

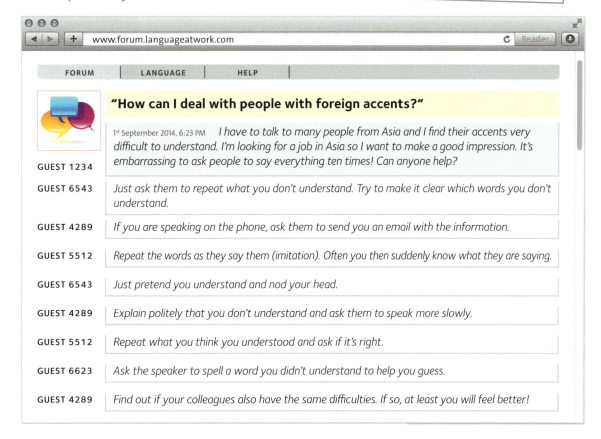

FORUM	**LANGUAGE**	**HELP**

"How can I deal with people with foreign accents?"

GUEST 1234 — 1ˢᵗ September 2014, 6:23 PM   *I have to talk to many people from Asia and I find their accents very difficult to understand. I'm looking for a job in Asia so I want to make a good impression. It's embarrassing to ask people to say everything ten times! Can anyone help?*

GUEST 6543 — *Just ask them to repeat what you don't understand. Try to make it clear which words you don't understand.*

GUEST 4289 — *If you are speaking on the phone, ask them to send you an email with the information.*

GUEST 5512 — *Repeat the words as they say them (imitation). Often you then suddenly know what they are saying.*

GUEST 6543 — *Just pretend you understand and nod your head.*

GUEST 4289 — *Explain politely that you don't understand and ask them to speak more slowly.*

GUEST 5512 — *Repeat what you think you understood and ask if it's right.*

GUEST 6623 — *Ask the speaker to spell a word you didn't understand to help you guess.*

GUEST 4289 — *Find out if your colleagues also have the same difficulties. If so, at least you will feel better!*

---

18   **A**   **06**))) Listen to the three speakers again. Which strategy in **17** would you use in each case?

B Now role-play a situation in which you don't understand what your partner says. Use the phrases below to help you.

- Could you possibly write that down for me?
- How do you spell that?
- I'm sorry, I didn't quite catch that. / I don't understand. / I missed that.
- Let me just check I understand: I should …
- Maybe you could send me an email with …
- So you mean, I should …

>  We often use "Could you …" to be polite.

19

A An effective orientation programme means a good start in a new job. Can you remember your own orientation? Think about the following questions.

What should an orientation programme include to
- make staff feel welcome?
- help them to see the company's vision?
- make them feel important to the company?
- give information about rules, company policy, etc.?
- prepare them for their job?
- let them take an active part?

B Read about Ashkan, an Iranian naval architect, and his orientation experiences in Iran, Scotland and Australia. What did he find particularly good about the orientation programmes? Who was in charge of the programmes?

All the companies organized short orientation programmes. I think it was two hours in Iran, three hours in Australia and one day in Scotland. In Australia and Scotland, the programme took place a month after I started work.

In Aberdeen and Perth, the HR manager was in charge and the main purpose was an introduction to the company – the structure, services, etc. – and to give us HR information. I mean information about working hours, holidays, company regulations, training courses, health and safety – things like that.

In Bandar Abbas, my boss was responsible for orientation so the focus was on company organization and my work. All the HR information was on the company intranet.

Each time we had a tour of the company, and there was a special lunch for all the new employees in Aberdeen.

I met everyone in the company on the first day in Perth and Bandar Abbas, so the orientation seemed like a welcome to the company. It wasn't really like that in Aberdeen. There it was more about getting information.

C 07 ») Listen to Qing speak about his experiences. He is a Chinese telecommunications engineer who worked for an American company in Germany and now works for a Chinese state-owned organization. What did his orientation programmes involve?

20

Project Work

Make some suggestions to help organize the ideal orientation programme for your company. Consider the points in **19A**, your own experience and what you learned from Ashkan and Qing. Use these phrases to help you present your ideas.

> It's important that the new employees …

> It's a good idea to …

> We should make sure that we …

> We want to …

> All new employees need to …

> It's essential to …

21 Grammar: prepositions

A Complete each sentence in as many ways as you can.

1 You can make a _____ impression on _____ by _____ .   2 Why don't you invite _____ to _____ ?

B Which preposition fits into all the sentences in each group (1–3)?

1 Make a note _____ everyone's name. Do you have any experience _____ managing projects? It's my job to find out the needs _____ our clients.

2 Our boss has worked here _____ over twenty years. What is important _____ the success of this project? I went _____ my first interview last week.

3 Take some sandwiches _____ you. We deal _____ customers all over Asia. I'm not very familiar _____ the new software.

C Rewrite the sentences from **B** by changing the underlined parts.

Example: Make a note of the date of the meeting.

---

22 Listening for specific information

A 08))) Listen to three people from Belgium talking about their lunch breaks. Match the speakers and the place.

speaker 1	A desk
speaker 2	B lunchroom
speaker 3	C canteen

B Listen again and make notes on how and why their lunch breaks are different.

C Complete these sentences without listening again. Listen to check if necessary.

1 The younger people in the company _____ _____ _____ longer lunch breaks.

2 Most _____ _____ bring a packed lunch and eat it in the canteen or _____ _____ desks.

3 If we have time, we go _____ _____ _____ or go shopping.

4 We come from nine different countries and speak English to each other _____ _____ _____ time.

5 Everyone wants to be first in the lunchroom to choose the sandwiches they _____ _____ !

---

23 Useful language

A What could you say in these situations?

1 You offer a co-worker a lift home.
2 You invite your colleagues to your home.
3 You ask a colleague to join you for lunch.

B How could your colleague reply? Choose suitable responses from this list.

Yes, OK. Just a minute, I have to finish this email, then we can go. ● Thanks, that would be a great help. ● I'd love to, but I'm only taking a short break today. ● Great! That sounds like fun. ● That's a nice idea. When do you want us to come?

Before the next class Ask people you know who work in other companies about the routines in their workplaces. Prepare to talk about what you find out.

For the next unit Imagine you are going to meet someone who knows nothing about your company. Write four sentences in English to explain what your company does. Bring the sentences to class.

02 Describing your company

1

A Look at the photos. What do you think these companies do?

A ☐ Malheur

B ☐ Messe Basel

C ☐ Metallbau Windeck

D ☐ Canada Wood

B 09))) Listen and complete the descriptions below. Then match them to the photos.

1 We _____ trade fairs in several locations in Switzerland. We _____ about 20,000 companies and over 2.3 million visitors to our exhibitions every year. Companies are often repeat customers, meaning we _____ good working relationships with them.

2 We _____ traditional methods to _____ specialist beers for the Belgian market and for export. We _____ in dark beers, for which we have won prizes.

3 We _____ high-quality metal doors, windows and facades. We _____ complete solutions from planning to construction. We _____ expert advice and _____ our doors and windows to suit our customers' needs.

4 We _____ the use of products made from Canadian wood. To do this, we offer training courses to help designers and builders, and _____ support for construction projects.

C Describe what your company does using sentences from the texts as models.

2

A Every industry has its own terminology. Use a dictionary to match the terms with the most likely company.

> Canada Wood ● Malheur ●
> Messe Basel ● Metallbau Windeck

> bottling ● brewing process ● exhibitor ● forest ●
> lumber ● stand ● steel ● welding

B Make a list of some terms in English which are specific to the industry you work in. Share your words in class. Which words are mentioned more than once?

3 Read these questions about a company.
Then match them to the answers.
What else could you ask?

How would you answer these questions about your own company?

1 Does the company do business in other countries?
2 Where is the head office?
3 Does the company have branch offices abroad?
4 How old is the company?
5 How many people work for the company?

A Yes, we do. The most important ones are in Tokyo and Dubai.
B It was founded in 1948.
C I think we employ about 200 people.
D Not yet, but we hope to start exporting to other European countries next year.
E We're based in Cologne.

4

Language Focus: asking for and giving information

If we want to find out or give some information, we often begin questions and answers with short phrases to make the conversation less direct.

A Asking for information:
 1 Can you tell me ... ?
 2 What do you know about ... ?

B Giving information:
 1 As far as I know, ...
 2 I'm pretty sure that ...

C If you are not quite sure of the answer, you can say:
 1 If I remember correctly, the company was founded in 1948.
 2 I may be wrong, but I think you can find John on the second floor.

You are going to find out more about two companies. Work with a partner:
Partner A → **File 3**, page **70**.   **Partner B** → **File 4**, page **72**.
Ask and answer questions to complete the two tables. Use the phrases above if you can.

> *If you don't know an exact figure, you can use expressions like:*
> *more than • over • nearly • about • less than*

---

5 **A** You may be interested in other facts and figures about a company. How would you ask for information on these topics?

annual production • annual sales • languages spoken • main competitors • main customers •
(*your own idea*)

B When you describe a company, the facts and figures you talk about depend on who you are talking to. Choose a person from the list and describe your company to them. Use the topics in **3** and **5A** to help you, or include your own ideas.

a new colleague • a customer • a supplier • a member of the public • a newspaper reporter

6

A Working conditions depend on the kind of company, national rules and, sometimes, on what staff prefer. Complete the comments on working hours with some of the expressions from the word cloud.

seasonal
home office **working hours** result-time
job share part-time full-time clock in face-time
working-time account teleworking 40-hour week overtime
shifts work-life balance flexible working hours
core time annual holiday

1 My company offers _____ with a _____ from 9.30 am to 3.30 pm.

2 I worked _____ after my son was born and did a _____ with a colleague,

but now I have a _____ job again.

3 Because our work is seasonal, we have a _____ and work less in the winter.

4 I work _____: one week I work days and the next week I work night shifts.

5 During very busy periods, nearly everyone in the company does _____.

6 I get 28 days _____ plus public holidays like Christmas, Easter, etc.

7

A 👥 What do you know about working hours in other companies and countries? Exchange ideas with a partner.

> SME = small and medium-sized enterprise 🔍

B 10)) Listen to four people talking about their workplaces. Who works where?

1 ◯ in a family-owned SME
2 ◯ in the public sector
3 ◯ in a non-profit-making organization
4 ◯ in a start-up

A	B	C	D
Agnes, Nairobi	Andreas, Lyon	Lukáš, Pilsen	Sandra, Brandenburg

C Look at the topics below and then listen again. Who does what? Write in the name(s).

international experience		set hours each day	
shift-work		seasonal work	
more than one job		owns the company	

8

👥 Read this blog post about time spent at work and productivity. Think about your own working hours. Then discuss the questions at the end of the text with a partner.

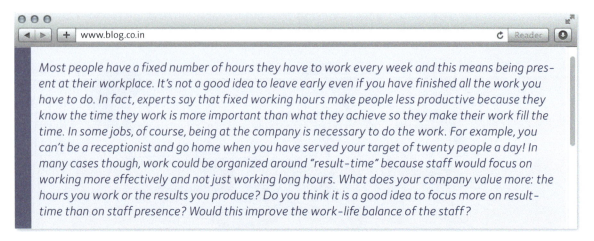

www.blog.co.in

Most people have a fixed number of hours they have to work every week and this means being present at their workplace. It's not a good idea to leave early even if you have finished all the work you have to do. In fact, experts say that fixed working hours make people less productive because they know the time they work is more important than what they achieve so they make their work fill the time. In some jobs, of course, being at the company is necessary to do the work. For example, you can't be a receptionist and go home when you have served your target of twenty people a day! In many cases though, work could be organized around "result-time" because staff would focus on working more effectively and not just working long hours. What does your company value more: the hours you work or the results you produce? Do you think it is a good idea to focus more on result-time than on staff presence? Would this improve the work-life balance of the staff?

9

A 11))) Listen to Andreas explaining what he does in more detail. Tick the correct answers.

1 Andreas's company …
 a ☐ manufactures products. b ☐ provides services.

2 The most important languages he uses at work are:
 a ☐ Danish. b ☐ Dutch. c ☐ English.
 d ☐ French. e ☐ German. f ☐ Spanish.

3 He works directly with …
 a ☐ business clients. b ☐ private customers. c ☐ manufacturers. d ☐ suppliers.

4 In the busiest periods, he deals with approximately …
 a ☐ 10 phone customers a day. b ☐ 25 customers a day. c ☐ 75 customers a day.

5 His company is under contract to …
 a ☐ the government. b ☐ insurance companies. c ☐ automobile clubs. d ☐ car manufacturers.

B Listen once more and tick the expressions Andreas uses to describe his job.

☐ I work in …
☐ I work for …
☐ I work with …
☐ I deal with …

☐ Our work involves …
☐ It's our job to …
☐ My work consists of …
☐ I do some …

☐ We coordinate …
☐ My role is also to …
☐ My position is …
☐ I check …

C What vocabulary is specific to Andreas's work?

roadside help

10

A What people do within a company depends on their department. Which departments do you think these people work in?

> 2 *I'm in charge of organizing training courses for our staff.*

> 1 *I'm responsible for finding a new supplier for our factory in India.*

> 3 *I focus on the most efficient way of moving goods from the factory to our customers.*

B Some terms are specific to certain departments. Match the words to the most likely department.

1 after-sales service
2 budget
3 equipment
4 recruitment
5 warehouse

A logistics
B HR
C finance
D marketing
E production

C Make a list of some terms you would need to describe your own work in English. Choose two or three of the terms that are more difficult and write sentences to show what they mean.

11 **Language Focus:** talking about regular, present and future activities

Which sentences refer to **a** what happens on a regular basis, **b** present activities or **c** plans for the future?

1. ◯ My job involves working closely with our new customers.
2. ◯ I deal with suppliers more often than with customers.
3. ◯ We're working on a new product using new production methods.
4. ◯ The company is opening a branch office in Singapore in two months.
5. ◯ We offer our customers complete solutions.
6. ◯ We're meeting our new project partners after the trade fair.
7. ◯ I'm working with an external consultant on this project.
8. ◯ The project is progressing according to schedule.
9. ◯ We're launching the new model at the trade fair in Basel.

12 **A** Look at the questions below. Which sentences from **11** could answer them?

1. ◯ What do you offer your customers?

2. ◯ How is your project progressing?

3. ◯ What are you working on at the moment?

B Now write your own questions for the other sentences in **11** and compare them with a partner.

C Write answers to all the questions which are relevant to your own work.

13 **A** 👥 Work with your partner and ask and answer some questions about your work.

Talk about:
- what you do on a regular basis.
- who you work with inside and outside the company.
- what you are working on at the moment.
- what definite plans you have for the future.

So, tell me a bit about your role in the company.

Well, I'm head of software development for our industrial clients.

B What is the same or similar about your jobs? What is different?

14 👥 Choose one of these situations and decide on the type of company. Look at the files for more details and give yourself time to prepare. Add any extra details that you need to say. Then role-play the conversation with a partner.

A meeting between a supplier and a potential customer.

Partner A → **File 5**, page 70.
Partner B → **File 6**, page 72.

If you prefer, choose a different situation which could happen in your own company.

Two people meet on a train or plane and start talking about their work.

Partner A → **File 7**, page 71.
Partner B → **File 8**, page 75.

Colleagues have come together for a weekly update meeting.

Partner A → **File 9**, page 74.
Partner B → **File 10**, page 73.

15 Read the questions and answers below. What problem does the person have? What would you do in his/her situation?

> *What would you do if you ask someone a question and don't understand the answer?*

> *I'd probably ask the person to repeat it.*

> *What would you do if you still didn't understand?*

> *Say thank you and go away.*

16

A A British footballer, Joey Barton, who played for a French team, gave interviews in France in which he spoke English with a French accent. Videos of this were uploaded to YouTube. Many people criticized him and made jokes about him for doing this. Was he wrong to speak like this? Why do you think he did it?

B 12)) Do you ever change the way you say something, depending on who you are speaking to? Listen to Agnes, an engineer, answering this question. Name three techniques she uses.

17

A Replace the words in blue with the expressions below that have a similar meaning. Which sentence in each pair do you find easier to understand?

am sorry but ● better ● finish on time ● found ● good enough ● know ● look again at ● may be possible ● sure ● want

1 I'm **confident** that we can **meet the deadline**.
2 We **are keen** to do business with your company.
3 Take a look at the **improved** version of the product.
4 I **regret that** your offer is not **acceptable**.
5 I think you **are aware** that we can't pay that price.
6 That **could work** for me.
7 We can **revisit** that topic once we agree on the basics.
8 Have you **identified** a solution to the problem?

B Read the phrases below. Then match them to their possible uses (a–d).

1 ◯ The point I'm making is that …
2 ◯ Now, let me tell you something about …
3 ◯ So, you mean that …
4 ◯ If anything isn't quite clear, please let me know.
5 ◯ Let me start by …
6 ◯ So, in other words, …
7 ◯ Maybe you have some questions at this point?
8 ◯ Are you saying that …?

a How can you check you have understood correctly?
b How can you check the person you are speaking to has understood what you said?
c How can you prepare your listener for what you are going to talk about?
d How can you say the same thing in different words?

C 👥 Work with a partner and role-play one of these situations or one of your choosing.

describing how something works ● making arrangements for a meeting ● explaining a problem with a piece of machinery

Partner A: Prepare to tell your partner, who is not a specialist, about the topic.
Partner B: You don't understand very much of what your partner is telling you.

18

A 13))) Listen to Martin from Penta-Electric giving an informal introduction to his company and his work. In the first part he talks about the company. Make a note of the phrases he uses for the following.

a   to start his presentation _____

b   to introduce himself _____

c   to introduce the company _____

d   to say what the company does _____

e   to move on to a description of his role in the company _____

B 14))) In the second part, Martin talks about his own job. Choose the best answers to these questions based on what he says. There may be more than one answer.

1   Who does he work with?
   a ☐ customers   b ☐ colleagues
   c ☐ business customers   d ☐ suppliers
   e ☐ government officials

2   How does he describe his work?
   a ☐ creative   b ☐ technical   c ☐ routine
   d ☐ varied   e ☐ challenging

3   What is important in his job?
   a ☐ communication skills
   b ☐ technical know-how   c ☐ precision
   d ☐ manual skills   e ☐ problem-solving skills

C Listen again and complete these sentences about Martin's work.

1   In his job, Martin ...   2   His job also involves ...

_____

_____

_____

19

Project Work

A Choose a scenario and prepare to give an informal presentation of your own company or your work. Look back through the unit to find the language which is most useful for the scenario you have chosen.

Scenario 1: A group of visitors from abroad have arrived and would like to hear what your company is really good at. You have been chosen to speak for the company.
Scenario 2: Present your department to a new colleague, explaining what you and other people in the department do.
Scenario 3: Present the project you are working on at the moment to one of the top managers of your company.

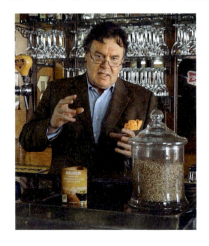

B Give a short presentation of 2 – 3 minutes. Try to do it without using your notes or only with 10 –12 keywords.

> **Film 1** 📽 If you want to see a different presentation of a company, watch the film in which Manu de Landtsheer describes his company, Malheur. Before you watch, turn to the exercises on page 95.

20

Grammar: talking about regular, present and future activities

Complete the conversation between Martin and Manu with the correct form of the verb in brackets.

Martin   A brewery sounds like an interesting place to work. So what _____ you _____ [1] (*enjoy*) most about your job?

Manu   Well, I _____ [2] (*spend*) a lot of time on the development of new products. At the moment, I _____ [3] (*plan*) a trip to visit our partners in Brazil to discuss some new ideas. Your job also _____ [4] (*sound*) very interesting.

Martin   Yes, it is. My job _____ [5] (*involve*) a lot of problem solving and that _____ [6] (*make*) it interesting.

Manu   What kind of companies _____ you _____ [7] (*deal*) with?

Martin   Many different kinds, but the project we _____ [8] (*work*) on now is for a pharmaceutical company. In fact, I _____ [9] (*meet*) the head of production later today.

21

Useful language

Use these sentence beginnings to write your own sentences. Choose one of these topics.

history of your company ● number of employees ● recent event at your company ● future event at your company

1   As far as I know, _____

2   I'm pretty sure _____

3   If I remember correctly, _____

4   I may be wrong but _____

22

Listening: what people do at work

15)) Listen to Anh Tuan talking about his company and job. Decide if these statements are true or false.

		T	F
1	Customers can call the helpline eight hours a day.	☐	☐
2	His employer knows when he arrives and leaves.	☐	☐
3	He had the same working conditions in Vietnam.	☐	☐
4	Their clients' problems are easy to solve.	☐	☐
5	He works mainly with German clients.	☐	☐

23

Vocabulary: prepositions

A   Fill in the missing prepositions.

1   I'm working _____ [1] a product _____ [2] the European market.

2   Our customer base consists _____ [3] many top companies because we have a reputation _____ [4] providing excellent service.

3   We specialize _____ [5] giving expert advice _____ [6] recycling.

B   Write your own sentences using the underlined phrases.

Before the next class   Think about some informal conversations you have had at work recently. What did you talk about? Who you were talking to? Bring the information to the next class.

For the next unit   What do you associate with *small talk*? What does the term mean? How important is it? Do you enjoy small talk? Prepare to explain your opinion in class.

03 Speaking informally

1

A What topics do you talk about during informal conversations at work? Read some answers to this question from around the world. Whose answer is closest to yours?

Camila, Brazil

- with colleagues: latest news, weekend
- with boss: latest news, weather
- with visitors: their company, events in city

Maria-Elisa, Chile

- with female colleagues: family, work issues
- with male colleagues: weekend, sport
- with boss: no informal conversation
- with visitors: weather, weekend

Angus, Scotland

- with colleagues: news stories, sport, TV
- with boss: the same as with colleagues
- with visitors: weather, driving conditions, work

Zakir, Bangladesh

- with colleagues: politics, our boss, sport
- with boss: sport, family, weather
- with visitors: weather, latest news

B When did you last have a conversation about any of these topics? Where did the conversations take place and who were you speaking to?

 Do you talk about political opinions or your salaries?

C What would you tell someone unfamiliar with your country about suitable topics of conversation at work?

Think about:
a which topics people often talk about in informal situations.
b which topics people prefer not to discuss (too personal, too sensitive or too boring).
c if it depends more on the individual than what is typical in their country.

Compare and discuss your answers with a partner.

2

A Cristian and Diego have both worked in several countries. Read about their experience of socializing with co-workers, both inside and outside the office.
Partner A → **File 11**, page 71.   **Partner B** → **File 12**, page 73.
Read the text and answer the questions in your file.

B  Partner A and Partner B work together. Exchange the information with your partner and compare what they said with your own experiences and opinions.

In my experience, …

When I worked in …

I noticed that …

I (don't) agree with …

3

A Choose the best option in these situations and explain your choices to a partner.

1 You see a co-worker in the corridor and he/she asks "How are you?". You answer by …
    a saying that you have a headache and a cold.
    b saying "Not bad, thanks".
    c smiling.

2 A co-worker comes to your office to introduce a visitor. You …
    a stand up, smile and shake the visitor's hand.
    b wave your hand and say how happy you are to meet him/her.
    c stand up and give him/her a hug.

B Would you react in a different way?

4

Thinking about your answers in **3**, decide what makes someone an effective communicator. Read these suggestions. Decide what is important (+) or not very important (–). Add your own ideas.

Having a sense of humour .... ◯   Having a wide vocabulary .... ◯

Being a good listener .... ◯   Having good body language .... ◯

Not worrying about mistakes .... ◯   Using correct grammar .... ◯

5

A Conversations often begin with some small talk. Read some conversation openers and fill in what you would expect to hear next.

> How can you translate the term 'small talk' into your own language? 🔍

1 By the way, my name is Camila Machado. – ....

2 Can I get you a cup of coffee? – ....

3 Did you have a good weekend? – ....

4 I believe we met at the conference last year. – ....

5 Beautiful day, isn't it? – ....

B **16**))) Listen and note down any words or phrases you hear which are the same or similar to your answers in **A**.

....

....

....

C Are the following true (T) or false (F) in your opinion? Compare and discuss your answers in class.

1 ◯ Small talk only takes place in informal situations.

2 ◯ We use a lot of fixed expressions and "routines" in small talk.

3 ◯ There are only a small number of small talk topics.

4 ◯ The purpose of small talk is to exchange information.

5 ◯ The purpose of small talk is to make people feel comfortable.

6 ◯ Small talk is usually a waste of time.

D **17**))) Listen to how two of the dialogues in **B** continue and decide what the situations are.

6

A When you are speaking informally, what you say depends on who you are speaking to and where you are. Match the speech bubbles to the situations.

a at reception
b at a conference
c colleagues at a meeting
d meeting a new colleague
e in the canteen with a visitor
f on the phone

☐ *I'm very pleased to finally meet you.*

☐ *How's the weather over there? It's very hot here.*

☐ *I'm not sure what to have. What would you recommend?*

☐ *I hope we finish on time. I've got another one of these to go to this afternoon.*

B How would you answer each one?

7

A **18**)) Read and listen to this conversation between Diego and a new colleague. Fill in the gaps while you listen.

Diego	Hello, _____ Carla, _____ ?
Carla	Oh, hello.
Diego	We met at the meeting this morning. I'm Diego.
Carla	Diego, yes _____ . Nice to see you again.
Diego	I'm just going to the canteen to get a coffee. Come with me and I'll show you where it is.
Carla	_____ ! ... _____ how long have you worked here?
Diego	For nearly two years now. It's a _____ .
Carla	I'm looking forward to it. My job is to coordinate a project with a new Italian partner.
Diego	_____ ? So I suppose you're Italian?
Carla	That's right. Originally, I'm from Pisa, but I've lived in Australia for over five years now. _____ ?
Diego	Well, I come from Quito originally, but I moved here two years ago, to start this job, in fact.
Carla	_____ ! Adelaide's a great place to live. I love living here.
Diego	_____ ! Me, too. _____ what did you do before?
Carla	I worked for a business consultancy – just a small company, but it gave me the chance to learn a lot.
Diego	_____ . Oh, I'm really sorry but I've got to go. I've got another meeting. But it was good to talk. See you later!
Carla	Of course. Thanks for the coffee!

B Read through the conversation again. How do Diego and Carla show that they are interested in their conversation and that they are listening to each other?

8

Language Focus: using adjectives and adverbs to keep a conversation going
We can use single words like the ones below to show interest and agreement.

absolutely ● certainly ● definitely ● excellent ● fantastic ● great ● really ● right

– Our department is having a party to celebrate finishing the project on time. – Really?
– I think it's a good idea to invite our new colleague to the meeting. – Absolutely.

To show agreement with a negative statement, we add *not*.
– It's not my job to do that. – Certainly not.

Look back at the conversation between Diego and Carla.
1 Which adjectives do they use to show they are happy with a suggestion? _____
2 Which adverbs do they use to show agreement? _____
3 Which adjectives and adverbs do they use to show interest? _____

9

A We often used fixed expressions to begin (B) and end (E) a conversation. Put these phrases into the correct category.

Hi, nice to see you again. .... ◯ Here you are. I was looking for you. .... ◯
Hello, it's very nice to meet you. .... ◯ I don't think we've met. .... ◯
You must be Camila Machado. .... ◯ Give me a call the next time you're in the area. .... ◯
Is that the time? .... ◯ It was great to see you again. .... ◯
Excuse me, aren't you Diego Vila from PTI? .... ◯ Would you excuse me, please? I have an
Well, it was nice to meet you. .... ◯ appointment in five minutes. .... ◯

B 👥 What would you say? Use phrases from **A** or similar expressions, and discuss with a partner.

What would you say if ...
1   you saw a colleague in the canteen?
2   you were at a conference and wanted to introduce yourself to a stranger?
3   you saw someone who you thought you recognized?
4   you wanted to finish the conversation very politely?

10

Language Focus: open and closed questions
We often start a conversation with a closed question but then continue with open, follow-up questions. Closed questions can be answered with one word or a short phrase. Open questions often begin with a question word (*why, how, what*, etc.) or a phrase like *Can you tell me about …?, What do you think about …?, What happened …?*

Did the meeting go well?   Yes.   *What did you discuss?*

1   Choose a suitable follow-up question from below to continue conversations 1 – 5 in a logical way.

Great. Can you tell me about the evening events? ● That's good news. When can we see the results? ●
I've never been there. What's it like? ● Why not? What happened? ● Same here. Who can we ask? ●
How does he like his new job? ● Where is it exactly? ● Why didn't you ask me for his number?

   1   Did you enjoy the office party? – No – _____

   2   Did you speak to Diego? – Yes – _____

   3   Is your head office in Rotterdam? – Yes – _____

   4   Is the project going well? – Yes – _____

   5   Do you know anything about next week's conference? – No – _____

2   👥 Choose one of the conversations and continue it. See how long you can keep it going.

11 Who do you have informal conversations with in English? What kind of informal situations do you experience at work? Tick the points which are true for you and add any which are missing.

clients ☐   colleagues ☐   project partners ☐   suppliers ☐ _____ ☐

on the telephone ☐   face-to-face ☐   regularly ☐   in the future ☐ _____ ☐

before/after meetings ☐   at trade fairs ☐   at social events ☐ _____ ☐

---

12 **A** The 3As of balanced conversations are: _answer_, _add_, _ask_. Read this conversation and mark the three parts in this way.

Diego	Hi Carla. How was your trip? You were in Sydney, weren't you?
Carla	Hi, there. It was great, thanks. Yes, I was in Sydney with some friends. Have you ever been?
Diego	Yes, I lived there for a short time, in fact, before I got this job. How long were you there?
Carla	Oh, only a week unfortunately. I'm too busy at the moment to take a longer holiday. By the way, could I ask you a favour?
Diego	Sure! I'm happy to help you if I can. What's the problem?
Carla	Well, I need some data about the project you're working on. Sara isn't in today so I can't ask her. Can I discuss this with you?

B How could you respond to these questions in a conversation about your own work? What information can you give about yourself? How can you move the focus to the other person?

1   Can you tell me something about your role in the company?
2   Will you be at the trade fair next week?
3   What are you working on at the moment?

---

13 **A** 👥 Choose one of the situations below or one you marked in **11**. Work with a partner and make up an informal conversation. Think about the following questions.

- How can you move from general topics to talking about work?
- What can you say to make the other person feel comfortable?
- What can you say to find out more about the other person's work?
- What information do you need to give about yourself and your work?
- What can you say to keep the conversation going?

Partner A and **Partner B** both have the same role. You are at a networking event at a trade fair and start talking to someone who works for a competitor. Try to find out as much as you can about how well his/her company is doing.	**Partner A**: You are having lunch in the office canteen with someone from the human resources department and want to find out if the company plans to make any changes. **Partner B**: You are from HR.
Partner A and **Partner B** both have the same role. You are visiting a company and are waiting at reception. You start talking to another visitor.	**Partner A**: It is the first day back at work after your holiday and you are talking to a colleague you don't know very well. You want to know what has happened while you were away. **Partner B**: You are the colleague.

B Role-play your conversation to the class or make a recording.

14

A 👥 Work in a group of four. Read your file and follow the instructions.
Partner A → File 13, page 71.   Partner B → File 14, page 73.
Partner C → File 15, page 75.   Partner D → File 16, page 77.

B Discuss how successful your conversation was and any problems you had.

15

A Discuss what you find out about conversation styles in different parts of the world from these pieces of information (anecdote, sayings, patterns of communication). Which match your personal communication style?

> **Anecdote**
> There were four participants at the project meeting: they were from Finland, Italy, Japan and Spain. Afterwards the Italian and the Finn were asked how the meeting went. The Italian said that everyone was very friendly, but only the Spanish manager seemed really enthusiastic about the project; the other two didn't say much. The Finn said that everyone was very friendly but that the Italian and the Spaniard didn't give him and his Japanese colleague a chance to speak.

Sayings

Don't just stand there, do something!
(*Western attitude*)

Don't just do something, stand there!
(*Eastern attitude*)

Patterns of communication

English-speaking: ―――――― ―――――― ―――――― ――――――
―――――― ―――――― ――――――

Spanish-speaking: ―――――― ―――――― ――――――
―――――― ―――――― ――――――

Asian: ―――――― ―――――― ――――――
―――――― ―――――― ――――――

B Describe a situation you have experienced when it was difficult to keep the conversation going (in any language). What do you think the reasons were?

cultural ● knowledge of the language ● lack of interest ● status of speakers ● personal

---

16

A In a successful conversation everyone who wants to speak should get the chance to do so.
Put these expressions into the correct column.

> We can use 'just' to make a message sound more friendly. 🔍

1 That's interesting.
2 How about you?
3 I see what you mean.
4 What do you think, (*name*)?
5 Can I just finish what I was saying?
6 There's just one more thing …
7 That's true.
8 I'd be interested to know what you think.

Keeping your turn	Encouraging someone else to speak	Showing you're listening

B Work in a group of three or four and talk about one of these topics (or your own idea).

a company social event ● holiday plans ● the journey to work ● a new project ● the next trade fair

Try to use as many of the expressions in **A** as you can and keep the conversation going for as long as you can.

17

A Read what some experts on workplace interaction say about socializing at work. Do you recognize your company in what they say?

Most people socialize to some extent with their co-workers, but a lot depends on the size of the company, the corporate culture and the department. Small companies are often less formal so staff interact a lot more with each other. Larger companies often have a more conservative atmosphere where staff are not encouraged to socialize with each other. Socializing inside the company is more important than meeting after work because that is where employees spend most of their time together. There should always be time for a coffee or lunch break where people can relax and talk about topics which are not connected to their work. Socializing is about just talking to others and taking a genuine interest in their lives. It doesn't have to take place during organized events or activities although company picnics, business lunches and other events which are sponsored by the company make it easier for a good workplace atmosphere to develop. However, be careful! Socializing can be bad for your career … if you do it wrong!

B What is your opinion of socializing at work?

A lot depends on …   … is more important than …   Companies should …   Most employees …

18

A Look at the poster of a law firm's entertainment committee. Does your company organize similar activities?

"Wine down" is a play on words. To "wind down" means to relax after working hard.

OFFICE QUIZ
Great prizes to be won!
WHERE? Balmoral Club
WHEN?   March 14th, from 7 pm

"WINE DOWN" *for Easter*
WHERE? conference room
WHEN?   April 18th, 4.30 – 8 pm

BRITISH HEART FOUNDATION
Charity bike ride • Fundraiser
WHERE? meeting in the reception area
WHEN?   May 24th, 2 pm

"WINE DOWN" *for Wimbledon*
WHERE? conference room
WHEN?   July 15th, 4.30 – 8 pm

B **19**)) Find out more about what the entertainment committee does and make a note of what you find out.

1   Who pays for the events the committee organizes?
2   One event is a bit different from the others. What is it and how is it different?
3   Why does the committee like the "wine downs"?
4   Why don't they have more variety in the programme?

19

Project Work

A Talk about the events mentioned in **18**. What sounds good to you? What would be suitable for your company?

B If your company doesn't have an entertainment committee, decide how you could get one started.

C Imagine you are members of the committee. Plan a programme for the next six months. What activities would be popular with the staff in your company? How would they be financed? Where could they take place? How many events should there be? Present your ideas to the class.

20 Listening for specific information

20)) Listen to three people talking and answer the questions.

1 Do Maria and Martin know each other?
2 Do Maria and Jakub know each other?
3 Where do you think they are?
4 Which two work in the same field?
5 Which comment is too personal for a first meeting?
6 Why does Martin leave?

21 Small talk

Complete the conversation with expressions below.

excuse me ● 15 minutes ● go ahead ● how did it ● how has ● how was ● I'm afraid ● let's get ● nice to see ● not bad

Martin Hi Rita. _____ [1] you again. Are you enjoying the conference?

Rita Hello Martin. _____ [2] I missed your talk. _____ [3] go?

Martin _____ [4] . The audience seemed to like it. _____ [5] your trip?

Rita OK, thanks. Look, _____ [6] a cup of coffee.

Martin Good idea. I have _____ [7] . _____ [8] the weather been in Hamburg?

Rita Terrible!

Martin Yes, that's what I thought. Please _____ [9] for a minute, I have to answer this call.

Rita No problem, _____ [10] .

22 Useful language

A Find different ways of completing each of these sentences from an informal conversation.

1 Can I get you _____ ?
2 How long have you _____ ?
3 It was nice to _____ .
4 Did you have _____ ?
5 How was _____ ?

B Choose the most suitable response to the questions in **A**.

1 a Yes, you can.   b No, I don't want one.   c That sounds great.
2 a For a long time.   b Very long.   c Yes, I have.
3 a That's right.   b It was my pleasure, too.   c Very nice, thanks.
4 a Yes, thanks.   b No.   c Certainly.
5 a I liked it.   b Fine, thanks.   c Definitely not.

Before the next class How would you explain to a visitor how to get to your company? Prepare to explain the best way from the main train station and/or airport in the next class.

For the next unit Find or draw a floor plan of your company. Take some photos of your own office/workshop/laboratory if possible. Bring everything to class.

04 Choosing a location

1 Is your company situated in a location similar to one of these? What are the advantages/disadvantages of locations like these?

- in a business park
- on an industrial estate
- in the countryside
- on the edge of town
- near a motorway exit
- in a side street

2

A Read the following questions about choosing a business location. Then match them with the criteria below.

brand image ● competitors ● costs ● crime ● customers and suppliers ● future growth ● government financial support ● local labour market

1 Does the area match the image of the company?
2 Does the area have the employees we need?
3 Can we apply for financial help from the state?
4 Can we afford to rent or buy the premises?
5 Is the location safe for our staff?
6 Is there extra space for future development?

B Rank the criteria mentioned in **A** from 1 (most important) to 7 (least important), using these phrases to help you.

… is the most important factor.

… is/are more important than …

… is/are more important for companies which …

… is/are as important as …

Of all of these factors, … is probably the least important.

C Present your ranking and explain your reasons. What other factors might be relevant?

D 21)) Now listen to two people discussing the topic. Do they share your opinion?
Listen again and match the phrases they use to introduce their opinions.

1	For	A	say that
2	If you	B	you the truth
3	I can't	C	ask me
4	to tell	D	make up my mind
5	I'd	E	me

3   **A**   Many company websites give directions on how to find them.
What information would be helpful to a first-time visitor from abroad?

B   **22))** Listen to some problems people have had trying to find the company they are visiting. If you are unsure how to get to your appointment, what questions can you ask?

C   What other problems might visitors have in this situation?

4

Language Focus: talking about options
Complete each question with a word from each row.

a good   better   best
b quick   quicker   quickest
c cheap   cheaper   cheapest

1   Is it _____ to take a taxi or the bus from the airport?
2   What's the _____ way to get to the airport from here?
3   Is there a _____ connection from here to the main station?

---

5   What directions and/or information would you give these visitors coming to your company for the first time? What are the best options?

Bill from the US
He only speaks English. First visit to this country. You met him in the US.

Eduardo from Brazil
He speaks Italian and French. He is new in his company.

Meifen from China
She speaks good English and some German. Regular visitor to Europe.

---

6   **A**   You have reached your destination. Role-play two encounters at the reception desk of a big company.
Partner A → File 17, page 74.   **Partner B** → File 18, page 78.

B   Why is neither conversation very successful? Do a better job and make up your own reception desk encounter using these sentences to help you. Add any details you like.

Receptionist
- Good morning, how can I help you?
- Who would you like to see?
- Do you have an appointment?
- I'll give … a call and let him/her know you're here.
- Please sign the visitors' list.
- Here's your security pass.
- Would you like to take a seat over there while you wait?
- … will be down in a moment.

Visitor
- My name is … I'm from …
- I have an appointment with … at …
- Could you let … know I'm here, please?
- Do I need to sign this list?

Host
- Welcome to …
- Sorry to keep you waiting.
- Did you have any trouble finding us?
- This way, please.

7

A Our working environment has an impact on our well-being at work. What is your workplace like?

an open-plan office • an office of my own • an individual cubicle • a shared office •
an open work station • a laboratory • the factory floor • a home office

B Read this article about attitudes to open-plan offices and cubicles. For what other reasons might a company choose a particular kind of workplace?

The working environment and layout of an office can have a huge impact on staff motivation and productivity. So what is the ideal working environment? Unfortunately, research on this topic produces conflicting results. Open-plan offices may be the modern way of working, but surveys in Scandinavia, Hong Kong and the USA show that staff who work in open-plan offices are less productive, more stressed and generally unhappier. They feel disturbed by other people's telephones and conversations, and would prefer to work in a cubicle with soundproof walls.

However, research at the University of California shows that many workers, particularly people working in situations where teamwork is important, say they are more creative and communicative in an open environment. So, while some people think an open-plan layout creates a better atmosphere, others are sure that cubicles make staff more productive. However, there is one thing everyone agrees on: an office of your own is a mark of higher status.

8

A 23)) Listen to Helen Guo talking about her workplace at the Shanghai office of Canada Wood. Complete the sentences.

1 When you _____ the entrance, you see the wooden structure immediately.

2 Our reception area is huge. This is something _____ companies in China.

3 From our client meeting rooms, we have a _____ the garden and the canal.

4 Our kitchen is _____ the building.

5 Our open-door policy is _____ style than typical Chinese.

B Listen again and make a note of how Helen compares her present and previous workplace.

9

Language Focus: making comparisons
Which sentences describe things that are **a** the same, **b** slightly different, **c** very different?
Underline the words which give you the answer.

1 ◯ An open-plan office is far better for communication between colleagues.

2 ◯ My office is a bit smaller than Helen's.

3 ◯ Is your company car park as big as this one?

4 ◯ I think a cubicle is as good as a private office.

5 ◯ It's a lot more expensive for the company if everyone has a private office.

10 Think about your own work. Compare your workplace to Helen's.

Helen's company is not as … as …

… is a bit bigger than …

The biggest difference is …

11 A tour of the company is often on the agenda for visitors and new employees. Different people may be taken to different places. What would you show? Fill out the table with the words below.

administration building ● break room ● CEO's office ● factory building ● factory floor ● fire escape ● first aid room ● lab ● HR department ● office supplies room ● loading/unloading dock ● lockers ● office building ● photocopying room ● post room ● production area ● server room ● showroom ● training centre ● warehouse ● workshops

government inspectors	members of the public	new employees	potential customers	visitors from head office

12

Language Focus: explaining where places are
Match the descriptions below with the positions (1–6) shown on this floor plan of an office building.

next to the conference room ● opposite the break room ● in front of the reception desk ● between the fire escape and the server room ● on the 2nd floor ● in the corridor

UK/India/ Australia	US/China/ Russia/Japan
ground floor	1st floor
1st floor	2nd floor

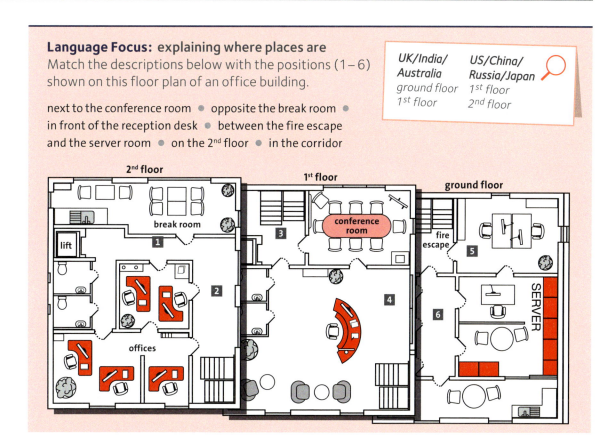

13 Describe the position of your office in as many different ways as possible.

It's next to …   It's between …   It's opposite …   It's on the …

14 **A** Label a floor plan of your company with terms from **11**.

B 👥 Work with a partner and take turns to describe where a particular room or area is. Can your partner guess the place?

If you don't have a floor plan of your company, use the one in 12 or draw your own.

15

A How can you signal that you are ready to begin a company tour? Match the sentence halves.

1 May I offer you something to drink
2 If you follow me,
3 We can make our way over to the factory
4 Shall we
5 We should get started

A if you're ready.
B get started?
C because there's a lot to see.
D before we start the tour?
E we can begin the tour.

B 24))) Listen to the beginning of a tour of a factory.
Who are the visitors?

a official inspectors
b members of the public
c potential customers

16

A Look through the list of phrases which are useful when showing visitors around.
Put them into a logical order using the timeline below.

| A 10:00 | B 10:10 | C XX:XX | D 10:15 | E 10:30 |
| F 10:40 | G 10:45 | H 11:00 | I 11:10 | J 11:20 |

1 ( ) So please just follow me down the stairs to the production area.
2 ( ) Just over there on the right, you can see our R&D labs.
3 ( ) Let's head back upstairs. Some refreshments are waiting for us.
4 ( ) If anyone would like to use the toilet before we start, they're over there.
5 ( ) As you can see, this is our production area.
6 ( ) I'd like to draw your attention to our new, highly innovative system.
7 ( ) Before we go in, please put on this protective clothing.
8 ( ) That brings us to the end of the tour for today. I hope it has been worthwhile.
9 ( ) Do you have any questions before we move on?
10 ( ) By the way, please feel free to ask questions at any time.

B 25))) Now listen and check your answers.

17 Complete the sentences with the words below. What function do they have during a company tour?

attention • everything • information • move • way

1 Would you like any more _____ about what we have seen so far?

2 Let me draw your _____ to the machine over here.

3 Please come this _____ .

4 We've seen just about _____ .

5 If there are no more questions, let's _____ on.

18

A What can make it difficult to understand spoken English? Complete these answers in as many ways as you can.

It can be difficult if the speaker _____

It can be difficult if I _____

19

A One of the keys to speaking clearly in English is pausing between groups of words within a sentence. Read the two examples aloud. Why is the second one easier to understand?

"When you come to our office it's better to take a taxi than waste time on public transport."

"When you come to our office || it's better to take a taxi || than waste time on public transport."

B When you pause in a sentence, you automatically stress certain words or parts of words.

"When you come to our **office** || it's better to take a **taxi** || than waste time on public **trans**port."

Read these sentences and practise pausing and stressing the blue words.

1 Ex**cuse** me, || which is the **nearest** station || to your **office**?
2 I'm sorry I'm **late**. || Has the **fac**tory tour || already **start**ed?
3 I'll give her a **call** || and let her **know** || that you're **here**.
4 Would you **like** || to take a **seat** over there || while you **wait**?

20

A It's possible to modify the meaning of a sentence by stressing different words. Match the sentences with their meanings.

1 I've made an appointment for **you** with Mr Aalto for tomorrow afternoon.

2 I've made an appointment for you with Mr **Aalto** for tomorrow afternoon.

3 I've made an appointment for you with Mr Aalto for **tomorrow** afternoon.

A (Not with Mr Oksanen)

B (Not this afternoon)

C (Not for your colleague)

B How would you say these sentences to stress the meanings given in brackets?

1 Can you tell me the way to reception? (I don't want to go to the cafeteria.)
2 I've started a new job. (My wife hasn't started a new job.)
3 I came to work by car today. (I usually come to work by bus.)
4 Is the meeting at ten? (Or is it taking place at eleven?)

21

26–27))) Helen from Shanghai is in Vancouver on a business trip. Listen to the voicemail message from a Canadian colleague and their follow-up call. Then answer the questions.

1 Why is Mark contacting Helen?
2 How does he suggest she gets to her appointment?
3 Why won't he come with her?
4 Why does he suggest meeting afterwards at the bus station?
5 Why didn't Helen answer his call?
6 Why can't she keep the appointment with Mr Altmann?

22

A **28**)) Read the introduction to a company tour below.
Then listen and mark the pauses (||) and underline (_) the words
or syllables that are stressed.

It's my pleasure to welcome you here today for a tour of our company.

For the next 30 minutes or so, I'll be showing you our production

department and our research and development labs.

B Now practise reading the text aloud.

23

A On a tour of a company you will probably pass various signs.
Match captions from this list to the correct sign.

1 In the event of fire, do not use this lift.
2 Ear protection must be worn.
3 Fire exit
4 Caution: Slippery when wet
5 Authorized personnel only
6 No smoking

A ◯   B ◯

C ◯   D ◯

B Think about the signs in your company. How would you explain them to a visitor who doesn't
understand the language?

1 We must _____

2 We mustn't _____

3 Be careful because _____

24

Project Work
Plan a tour of your company. Agree on the following points
before you start.

1 Who are the visitors?
2 What parts of the company do you want to show them?
3 How long is the tour?
4 Do you want to offer any refreshments or arrange a special event?

Using the timeline in **16** as an example, make your own timeline and add any phrases you
think will be useful at each point.

Practise what you are going to say and how you are going to say it. Make it as easy as
possible for your visitors to understand you by practising pausing in the right places and
putting stress on the important words. Practise the tour using your text, then try to say it
without the text.

Now take your visitors on the
tour!

Film 2 🎬 If you want to see a real company tour,
watch the film in which Oliver Windeck gives a
tour of his company, Metallbau Windeck. Before
you watch, turn to the exercises on page 98.

25

Grammar: comparisons

Complete the sentences with the most suitable expression.

a bit closer to ● as good as ● more careful ● more impressive ● most expensive ● much better

1   Renting office space in the city centre is the _____ option.

2   I think it's a _____ idea to move to a location in a business park.

3   Our new office is _____ my home than the old one.

4   Staff should be _____ with the new equipment.

5   The new machines are a lot _____ than I expected.

6   Why are you complaining? I think your office is _____ mine.

26

Grammar: describing positions

Complete these sentences in any way you wish.

1   _____ opposite the _____

2   _____ in front of _____

3   _____ next to the _____

4   _____ at the end of _____

5   _____ on the right of _____

6   _____ between the _____

27

Useful language

A When would you say this? Put questions 1 – 6 into the most suitable category.

Asking for directions	At reception	During a company tour

1   Shall we head back to my office?
2   What's the quickest way to the station?
3   Would you like to wait over there for her?
4   Where can I park my car?
5   What was the name again, please?
6   Have I answered all your questions?

Before the next class Make a note of the content of two emails you write and two telephone calls you make before the next class. Prepare to talk about them in class.

B If someone said this to you, how would you reply?

1   Would you like something to drink?
2   What's the best way to get to your office from the station?
3   Where's the finance department?

For the next unit When is an email the best way to communicate and when is it better to use the phone? Answer the question using some examples from your own work. Prepare to discuss this in class.

05 Communicating professionally

1

A Look at these survey results from 2012. Do you think the forecast has come true?

Which will be, in your opinion, the most important instrument in business communication by 2015?

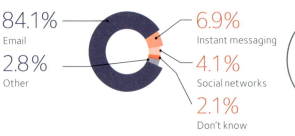

84.1%
Email

2.8%
Other

6.9%
Instant messaging

4.1%
Social networks

2.1%
Don't know

B Draw a pie chart showing how much time you spend using different communication tools at work. Compare with a partner. Discuss if and how you think this may change over the next five years.

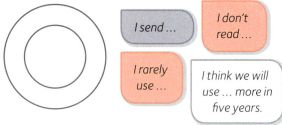

I send …   *I don't read …*   *I rarely use …*   *I think we will use … more in five years.*

2

A Would your life be better or worse without email? Think of reasons to support each answer.

B Now read a blog on the future of email and discuss which points and opinions you agree or disagree with.

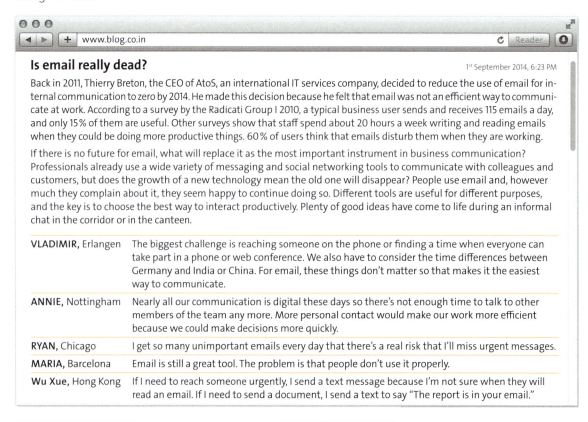

www.blog.co.in

Is email really dead?

1st September 2014, 6:23 PM

Back in 2011, Thierry Breton, the CEO of AtoS, an international IT services company, decided to reduce the use of email for internal communication to zero by 2014. He made this decision because he felt that email was not an efficient way to communicate at work. According to a survey by the Radicati Group I 2010, a typical business user sends and receives 115 emails a day, and only 15% of them are useful. Other surveys show that staff spend about 20 hours a week writing and reading emails when they could be doing more productive things. 60% of users think that emails disturb them when they are working.

If there is no future for email, what will replace it as the most important instrument in business communication? Professionals already use a wide variety of messaging and social networking tools to communicate with colleagues and customers, but does the growth of a new technology mean the old one will disappear? People use email and, however much they complain about it, they seem happy to continue doing so. Different tools are useful for different purposes, and the key is to choose the best way to interact productively. Plenty of good ideas have come to life during an informal chat in the corridor or in the canteen.

VLADIMIR, Erlangen	The biggest challenge is reaching someone on the phone or finding a time when everyone can take part in a phone or web conference. We also have to consider the time differences between Germany and India or China. For email, these things don't matter so that makes it the easiest way to communicate.
ANNIE, Nottingham	Nearly all our communication is digital these days so there's not enough time to talk to other members of the team any more. More personal contact would make our work more efficient because we could make decisions more quickly.
RYAN, Chicago	I get so many unimportant emails every day that there's a real risk that I'll miss urgent messages.
MARIA, Barcelona	Email is still a great tool. The problem is that people don't use it properly.
Wu Xue, Hong Kong	If I need to reach someone urgently, I send a text message because I'm not sure when they will read an email. If I need to send a document, I send a text to say "The report is in your email."

What … says is right.   *I don't think that …*   *It's quite true that …*   *… doesn't sound right to me.*

3 The type of communication we choose depends on the situation and what we need. When are these communication channels most suitable?

1	landline phone call	5	face-to-face meeting (two people)
2	mobile phone call	6	face-to-face meeting (group)
3	text message	7	email
4	instant message	8	phone conference

9 web meeting/video conference
10 letter

If something is very urgent, … is the best option.

If members of the team are based in Asia, …

If I want to confirm some arrangements, …

4

Language Focus: when and how we do things
Read these sentences and pay attention to the position of the adverbs.

I **often** receive as many as 50 emails a day.

From time to time I have to write letters to customers.
I have to write letters to customers **from time to time**.

My boss types **slowly**.

But: I am **sometimes** slow at replying to emails.
We have **never** considered becoming a paperless office. (after "be" and auxiliary verbs).

Are these sentences correct? Correct any that are wrong.
1 We rarely send text messages.
2 I write never emails to my colleagues.
3 Tomorrow we will get new software so we can instant message one another.
4 I spend usually two hours a day writing emails.

5

A **29**)) Katrin is the HR Manager at Messe Basel. Look at the pie charts showing how often she uses different types of communication. Listen to what she says about them.
Use some of the expressions below to say how often she uses the different channels.

a lot ● always ● every day ● from time to time ● hardly ever ● never ● not very often ●
often ● rarely ● sometimes ● usually

Internal and external communication

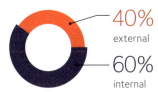

40% external
60% internal

Most common types of communication

30% email
40% face-to-face
20% phone
10% video/phone conference

B 👥 Listen again and give the reason why Katrin chooses each type of communication. Now discuss the use of different communication channels with a partner. Why does he/she choose them? Compare his/her reasons to what Katrin says.

C What impact does the language you speak have on the communication channels you choose? Read what Katrin says about her choices and tell your partner what you do in similar situations.

In general, I choose the most suitable communication channel for the purpose, of course, but if I have to contact someone in English or French, I usually prefer to speak to them personally or on the phone because that's easier for me than writing, but I always send an email if someone needs written confirmation.

6

A Which of these expressions can you use in **a** phone calls, **b** emails or **c** both?

1 ◯ Is this a good time to call?

2 ◯ I'm afraid I have to go to a meeting now.

3 ◯ Thanks for your quick reply.

4 ◯ Please let me know if you have any further questions.

5 ◯ Is this a good time to talk?

6 ◯ It'd be great if you could ...

7 ◯ Thanks for getting back to me so quickly.

8 ◯ You'll be pleased to hear that ...

9 ◯ It was nice talking to you.

10 ◯ I'll get back to you as soon as I can.

11 ◯ Do you have a moment?

12 ◯ Just a quick ... to let you know that ...

13 ◯ Thank you in advance.

14 ◯ I'm really sorry, but ...

B Which expressions can you use at or near the beginning of a call or email, and which at or near the end? Write down the numbers of the relevant sentences.

Beginning: _____   End: _____

C Choose three or four of the expressions from **A** which you could use at work. Complete or change them so they are relevant for you.

7

Complete these sentences in a way which is relevant to your work situation. How could you use them – on the phone, in an email or both?

1 Explaining the purpose
I'm calling about ...

2 Asking for action
I'd be very grateful if you could ...

3 Giving good news
You'll be pleased to hear that ...

4 Sending documents
Please find attached a(n) ...

5 Apologizing
I'm really sorry, but ...

6 Making arrangements
Could I give you a call next week to ...?

8

👥 When you use any kind of communication technology, you can have technical problems. Choose one of the problems below and discuss with a partner what you would say or write in this situation. Make up any details you like.

I'm sorry, I can't hear you very well.

I'll have to call you back.

My battery is very low.

Could you resend the email?

Problem 1
You were speaking to someone when the conversation was cut off. You call back but cannot hear the person very well. Your phone battery is very low so you don't have much time to talk.

Problem 2
You sent an email last week asking for a quick reply. You had some technical problems with your own email account a few days ago. You're not sure if your email arrived or if you just haven't received a reply yet.

9

A **30))** In a normal week at work, Katrin makes and receives lots of different phone calls and sometimes takes part in video conference calls. Listen and complete parts of some of her conversations.

1 **Katrin** I'm phoning _____ _____ _____ [1]

that your interview went very well. We were very _____

_____ [2] your knowledge of the whole field of logistics.

Bella I'm happy _____ _____ [3] that. I've always

enjoyed working in this area.

Katrin That's the impression we had, too. You'll get written

_____ [4] of our job offer in the post _____

_____ [5] of the week.

2 **Pedro** Great to _____ _____ _____ [1], Katrin. How's the weather in Basel?

Katrin A bit cloudy, but quite warm. Not as good as in Miami, I'm sure!

Pedro You're probably _____ [2] about that! Now, let's _____ _____ [3]. Can

you see the slides? I'd like to _____ _____ _____ [4] how far we've

got with our contracts for the temporary employees.

Katrin Yes, I can see the slides, but I can't hear you very well.

Pedro _____ [5] better?

3 **Katrin** Everyone in the second group is very busy tomorrow so we'd like _____ _____ [1]

our lesson until Friday. _____ _____ _____ [2] possible?

Clark Well, it depends _____ [3] we can meet. I'm in Lörrach on Friday

morning, but I'll be back in Basel _____ [4] 4.30 pm.

Katrin That sounds fine. I'll check with everyone and will _____ [5]

by this evening, OK?

B Listen again. What is the purpose of each phone call?

1 _____ 2 _____ 3 _____

C 👥 Choose one of the conversations and complete it by writing a beginning and an end. Role-play the finished dialogue.

10

> **Language Focus:** specific situations and general rules
> Which sentence refers to **a** a specific situation or **b** a general rule? Notice the different verb forms.
>
> If you **want** to reach someone urgently, it's a good idea to phone their mobile number.
> I'**ll give** you a call tomorrow if I'**m going** to be late.
>
> Complete these statements with the correct form of the verb.
>
> 1 I always _____ (arrange) to call if we have a problem we need to solve quickly.
>
> 2 If you don't have his mobile number, it _____ (be) very difficult to reach him before the meeting.
>
> 3 I'm sure she _____ (not forget) to return your call if you send her an email to remind her.
>
> 4 If I need quick feedback on a document, I often _____ (phone) my team.

11

A Dirk Jakob works for an agency which provides business support. Look at the two emails he's received. Which email is more informal? Why do you think so?

Dear Mr Jakob, **Email 1**

While going through the documents from the recent Energy 2020 Conference, we noticed that our company is no longer listed in the research and development section. Does this mean that we are no longer part of the regional energy group? If that is the case, why has this happened?

We would be very grateful for some feedback on this issue. Thank you.

Best Regards,

Matthias Neumann

Windflow GmbH

Dear all **Email 2**

After the meeting yesterday we talked about going to a sushi restaurant together. There are three sushi places in Bonn. @Dirk, we don't have to meet in Bonn if you have a better suggestion.

If you're up for it, we need to decide on a date first of all. I'll be on holiday from June 12th so I hope we can find a date which suits everyone before that. Here's a link to the doodle poll:

http://doodle.com/sushi

I'm looking forward to seeing your votes by next Monday at the latest :)

Best

Manya

B Now answer these questions.

Email 1
1 How would you describe the tone of the email: **a** angry, **b** surprised, **c** pleased? What makes you think that?
2 What does Matthias Neumann want?
3 How do you think Dirk should react?

Email 2
4 Who is Manya writing to? What is the main purpose of her email?
5 What other information do we find out and what can we guess?

C The writers don't use standard phrases to explain why they are writing. Read the emails again and complete these sentences to give the reason for writing and to request action or information.

Email 1
We are writing to …
We would like to know …

Email 2
I'm writing to …
Please …

12

A Now read the reply to email 1 and complete the text with verbs below.

apply ● clarify ● give ● hear ● left ● operate ● referring ● suit ● worry

B Why do you think Dirk wants to speak to Matthias Neumann on the phone? What do you think he will say? Work with a partner to write the telephone conversation.

Dear Mr Neumann,

Thank you for your email.

Although I am not sure which documents you are _____[1] to, you will be pleased to _____[2] that there is no reason to _____[3]. All companies in our region which _____[4] in the energy sector, including, of course Windflow GmbH, are in the group. Companies do not have to _____[5] for membership so cannot be _____[6] out.

I will be out of the office tomorrow, but would like to _____[7] you a call on Thursday to _____[8] this issue. Would 11 am _____[9] you?

I am sorry for any misunderstanding.

Best regards,

Dirk Jakob

---

13 Write the follow-up email Manya sent after getting the results of the doodle poll. Add any details you want and compare your version with a partner.
(If you like, when you have finished, turn to **File 19** → page 74 to see the answer she sent.)

14 Read the start of these real emails from various countries. Discuss the differences you notice in **a** the greetings, **b** the choice of words and **c** the context.

> Compare them with emails you have received from other countries.

> 1 Dear members,
>
> I hope this email will find you in good health and great happiness.
>
> *(invitation to a pan-Asia conference, Korea)*

> 2 Dear liz griffin,
>
> We hope this email finds you in great joy and health! Here is the latest issue of our newsletter for you and your loved ones.
>
> *(reply to request for a professional newsletter, India)*

> 3 Dear Alison Buckley,
>
> Thank you for taking the time to inform me of the unacceptable behaviour of our drivers on the no. 54 bus service.
>
> *(reply to a complaint from customer service of a bus company, UK)*

> 4 Sharon,
>
> So great to hear from you! I think this looks like a great package that you are offering.
>
> *(reply to an enquiry about hotel facilities for a conference, US)*

> 5 Dear Miriam,
>
> Thanks for your order for documents at our online shop.
>
> *(query from a UK university after an online purchase)*

> 6 Dear Mrs Camila,
>
> I hope this email finds you well. Please find attached a copy of the report you requested.
>
> *(reply to a request for a project report, Brazil)*

> When writing emails in English, non-native speakers often prefer to use the norms of writing in their own language.

15 **A** A visitor is coming to your company tomorrow and it's your job to show them around. Something unexpected has happened so you need to find a colleague who can take over for you. Compare two emails sent in this situation. What is the tone in each of the emails? Mark the parts of the text which back up your answer.

> Hello Lars,
>
> I have an appointment at the Ministry tomorrow to present the new wind energy project. You know yourself that there is no way I can postpone this. Unfortunately the delegation from Poland is also arriving tomorrow morning so would you welcome them for me and show them around the office? I'll send you some details about the delegation, our co-operation so far, etc. by 3pm.
>
> It shouldn't be too much trouble, remember Jan Laskowski speaks fluent Polish and will translate if necessary.
>
> I'd be very grateful if you could help me out. BTW, I'll let you win the next time we go bowling :)
>
> Best,
>
> Dirk

> Chen Chun,
>
> I have an appointment with the General Manager of our partner company in Wuhan tomorrow morning. However, I just got an urgent request from our General Manager to attend a conference in Haikou tomorrow. I have to drive over there this afternoon and cannot receive Mr Wang personally.
>
> Would it be possible for you to meet him on my behalf?
>
> Thanks a lot in advance.
>
> Liu Yang

B Now imagine that you are in this situation. Write an email and compare with a partner. What differences and similarities do you notice between your email and the emails in **A**?

16 Based on the emails on this page and your own experience, do you think you should adapt your written style for contacts abroad? What changes can or do you make? What do you not change?

17

A Despite people's desire to go digital (see chart), paperless offices are still unusual. Make two lists about **a** when it is better to use paper, and **b** when it is better to use digital tools.

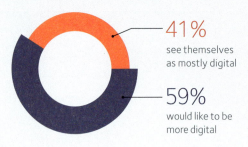

41%
see themselves
as mostly digital

59%
would like to be
more digital

" THIS IS WHAT I MISS MOST ABOUT THE OFFICE GOING PAPERLESS. "

B What arguments can you think of to agree or disagree with these statements?

1 If you use a lot of paper, you increase costs.
2 Too much paper is bad for productivity.
3 Paper documentation is less secure.

4 A digital company can attract the best employees.
5 Going digital is the only way to become a green company.

---

18 Read what employees from different kinds of companies say about the paperless office. Which one sounds most like your company? How is it similar or different?

> We're not very strict about it, but we re-use all paper from the fax machine that has been printed on one side for informal paperwork. We ask staff to only print out emails if it's really necessary. *Li Ying, Shanghai*

> Especially in our business, the paperless office is not only encouraged but also a necessity. Because we work from different geographic locations on the same centralised databases, we hardly print out anything at all. *Jan, Lyon*

> I think the paperless office is a very good idea but it has never had the chance to succeed in our company. There are no regulations or incentives to promote a paperless office although we have everything we need for such a change: desktop computers, tablets, mobile phones, a shared information structure, etc. *Annette, Cologne*

> If you want to be paperless, you need to scan every paper coming in and going out (letter, fax, invoice, etc.) and then give it to the person who works on it. That's a lot more work for the secretary, but no less work for the person responsible. For some documents like contracts or invoices you need the originals on paper, too, so you have to work with two files. *Simon, Berlin*

> There are no printers in the offices. We don't have any posters or notice boards so all information is on digital displays in the open areas. The only documents which are always on paper are contracts. *Elodie, Brussels*

> Most standard processes are paperless (e-purchasing, project management, holiday plans, timesheets, etc.). In fact, most important documents are made available electronically without a signature on paper. In most cases, we exchange data by email or using network drives. *Erika, Linz*

19

Project Work

Make a list of the advantages and disadvantages for your company of going or being paperless.

Depending on the situation in your company, choose project A or project B.

Project A
If you work in a paperless office, create a presentation to explain how it works and why it is such a good (or bad) idea.

Project B
If you work in a company which is a long way from being paperless, develop a strategy to help the company reach this goal.

20

Grammar: prepositions

Complete the sentences from emails and phone calls with the correct preposition.
In some cases more than one answer is possible.

about ● for (2x) ● from ● of ● on (2x) ● to

1 I'm calling _____ the interviews on Thursday.

2 Here is the information you asked _____ .

3 Can I get back _____ you later today?

4 I'm out _____ the office until March 15th.

5 We are very sorry _____ the delay in answering your query.

6 Let's decide _____ a date for the meeting, shall we?

7 I look forward to hearing _____ you soon.

8 I'll send you my feedback _____ your suggestion next week.

21

Grammar: adverbs

Put the adverbs of frequency into the correct position or positions in the sentence.

1 (often)   I take part in video conferences.
2 (never)   my boss is late for departmental meetings.
3 (from time to time) we have meetings to discuss company strategy.
4 (rarely)   I am away on business.
5 (every month)   I organize a project meeting.

22

Listening: voicemail messages

31)) Listen to some voicemail messages and note down these
pieces of information:

● name of caller

● reason for call

● next steps (call back/email?)

23

Useful language

Think about the kinds of emails you
write and phone calls you make in your
job. Make a list of useful phrases you
have learned in this unit in categories
like these: greeting people, opening
phrases, thanking people, asking for
information, etc.

Before the next class What image do you
think foreigners have of your country and
working habits there? How true do you think that
image is? Think about these questions and
prepare to give your opinion.

For the next unit Make a list of what, in your
opinion, are the dos and don'ts of effective
teamwork.

06 Working as a team

1

A Look at two images from an exhibition called *East meets West* and choose the most suitable title for each one. What does each image suggest about how people think or what they do?

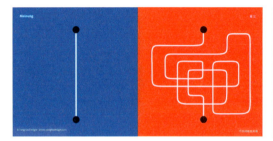 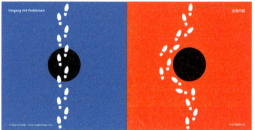

boss ● dealing with problems ● innovation ● opinion ● networking ● newcomer

B Compare your ideas to some other interpretations of the pictures. Exchange information with your partners. Did you interpret the pictures in the same way? How true do you think the images are?

Partner A → **File 20**, page 75.   **Partner B** → **File 21**, page 77.

2

A Read these short profiles of people from three different continents. Are they more "eastern" or "western"? Why do you think so?

Maurício is Brazilian. He trained as a mechanical engineer in Sao Paulo. He has worked as a technical translator and is now a patent engineer.

Merlene comes from Northern Ireland and works in HR. Before she came to Germany, she worked in the human resources department of a pharmaceutical company in Belfast.

Sarfaraz is from Pakistan, where he worked in the marketing department of a cement company in Karachi. Now he works at an institute for information systems in Germany.

B 32)) Listen to what Maurício, Merlene and Sarfaraz say about business culture in their home countries. Were your ideas in **A** right?

C How would you describe your own culture? Compare your ideas in class.

3

A Different cultures have different attitudes to time. What difference in behaviour do these images show?

> *on time = exactly on schedule*
> *in time = not too late*

B Evaluate each of the situations below. Choose the ending which is true for you or your culture. Do you completely agree with the statement?

1 Business meetings, appointments and presentations should ...
    a always start and finish on time.   b be flexible because other things may happen and cause delays.

2 If you arrive late for a meeting, you should ...
    a apologize and explain why.   b come in quietly and sit down.

C What effects can differences in attitude to punctuality have on teamwork?

4

Language Focus: what I (would) do if ...
Which sentences refer to a situation which **a** really happens from time to time and **b** could happen but doesn't happen often?

1 I would be surprised if my boss asked me to cancel my holiday because of a deadline.
2 If I'm not at my desk, a colleague answers my phone.
3 If my boss arrived late for a meeting, I wouldn't comment.
4 If I am late for a meeting, I think of a good excuse.
5 It's impossible to be on time if the traffic is very bad.
6 If my team members worked too slowly all the time, I would call a meeting to discuss the problem.

In sentences describing a situation which happens from time to time, you can replace *if* with *when*.

When I'm not at my desk, a colleague answers my phone.

5

33)) Listen to four people talking about time. What do they say about being on time?

6

A Match the situations with the most likely apology / explanation.

1 You are on the way to a meeting and know you will be late.
2 You arrive a few minutes late for a meeting.
3 You arrive half an hour late for work.
4 You were not in your office for a scheduled phone call.
5 You are on the way to an appointment in a city where bad traffic jams are the norm.

A I left my mobile in the car last night so I didn't hear the alarm.
B The traffic is terrible. I'm afraid I'll be a bit late so just start without me.
C I'm so sorry I wasn't at my desk when you called. Is this a good time to talk?
D I'm running late. I'll be with you in about an hour.
E I'm sorry I'm late. I had an important customer on the phone.

B Imagine you are late for work, for a meeting or for a scheduled phone call. How would you apologize and explain why you are late? What reasons would you give?

7

34)) Victoria is a software developer from Argentina who is working in Germany. Her project leader has asked her to arrange a web meeting for the development team. Read and complete the telephone conversation. Then listen and check.

V Hello Gustavo, this is Vicky. How are you?

G _____ ¹ , thanks. It's _____ ² from you. _____ ³ in Stuttgart?

V Very _____ ⁴ , but summer's coming so that makes life more fun. Remember that nice restaurant near the park we went to when _____ ⁵ here?

G Yeah, I remember.

V We had a working lunch there yesterday. _____ ⁶ I'm calling. In fact, Peter Wegner asked me _____ ⁷ a web meeting for a project update.

G OK, that's a _____ ⁸ because we have a few questions. The last meeting was very early in the morning here so would it be possible _____ ⁹ which is during our normal working hours this time?

V Sure, if we can find a good time. He asked me to suggest this Thursday. So, _____ ¹⁰ 3 pm here? That's 10 am with you, right?

G The time is perfect, but Friday would _____ ¹¹ because we're meeting a client ¹² 10 am on Thursday.

V Let _____ ¹³ our calendar. It looks OK, but I think Melanie is doing something _____ ¹⁴ . I'll ask her and then I'll send an email confirming the details. OK?

8

Language Focus: talking about arrangements
Which of these sentences refers to **a** what someone is doing now or **b** a fixed arrangement in the future?
1 ◯ I'm meeting my project partners this afternoon.
2 ◯ What are you doing tomorrow?
3 ◯ I'm running late.
4 ◯ I'm calling about our appointment next week.

How is *will* + verb used in these sentences?
1 I'll give her a call to check if she's available.
2 I'll find that out for you and call you back.
3 I'll see what I can do.

> *Today is Wednesday:*
> *this Friday = this week*
> *next Friday = next week*

9

Imagine that no one can come to the next English class so you have to change the date. Check your own schedule to find the two most suitable times for you. Now try to agree on a date for the next class. If someone suggests a time which is impossible for you, explain why you can't make it.

Suggesting a time
• How about 3 pm on Friday?
• Would 10.30 suit you for our meeting?
• Could I call you at 11 tomorrow?
• We could meet before/after lunch.
• Do you have time on Tuesday morning/afternoon?

Agreeing/Disagreeing
• That would be fine.
• Yes, that works for me.
• I'm sorry, I have another meeting then.
• No, I'm afraid that will be difficult.

Changing or suggesting a new time
• I'm free from 4 if that's OK for you.
• Could we make it 4.30 instead of 4?
• What about the same time but on Thursday?
• I'm sorry, but I can't make our meeting after all.
• I'm afraid I'm going to have to cancel.
• Could we bring the meeting forward/push the meeting back?
• Could we reschedule?

10

A 👥 What kind of meetings do you attend? Compare your answers with a partner.

departmental meetings ● team meetings ● face-to-face meetings ● video conferences ●
web meetings ● phone conferences ● informal meetings

B **35** 🔊 Listen to Victoria talking about the last meeting she attended
and answer the questions.

a What type of meeting was it?
b Who was there?
c What was the purpose of the meeting?

d What was on the agenda?
e What were the outcomes of
   the meeting?

C 👥 With a partner, take turns to describe a meeting you took part in recently. Then look at the
questions in **B**. Can you answer all of them about your partner's meeting?

11

A What are the main differences between face-to-face meetings and virtual meetings?

> *It's difficult to know if everyone is paying attention in a virtual meeting.*

> *It's easier to understand people in face-to-face meetings.*

B What do people say in meetings? Sort the following statements and questions (1–10) into the table.

1 Can you all hear me?
2 Are we all here?
3 What time is it in Rio?
4 Let's start.

5 Can you take us through the next
   point on the agenda, Melanie?
6 Please write your ideas or questions
   in the chatbox.
7 The line is very bad today.

8 It's great to see you all again.
9 Let me give everyone a copy
   of the report.
10 Good afternoon – and good
   morning to Gustavo's team!

face-to-face meetings	virtual meetings	both kinds

C Can you think of any other things people might say in virtual meetings but not face-to-face?

---

12 Read how Peter Wegner started the meeting Victoria talked about in **10**. Then practise starting a
meeting you often take part in using Peter's introduction as a guide.

I think we're all here so let's get started. Thank you all for being here on time today. I know we are all very busy.
So, does everyone have a copy of the agenda? As you can see, the purpose of the meeting is a project update so
we all know the status of the software. But before we discuss the first point, I'd like everyone to tell us something
about what they've been doing. Then we can focus on the problems with the time management software.

13

A Deadlines and schedules are often a topic in meetings. The wrong time preposition or phrase
can cause confusion. Complete the sentences with expressions from below.

as soon as ● at the end ● before ● by ● in the end ● on a daily/weekly basis ● once a …

1 I'm handing in the report _____ of the month.
2 Can you give that to me _____ Friday at the latest, please?
3 We missed the deadline but everything will be OK _____, I'm sure.
4 This is a difficult project so we have video conferences _____ month.

B Use some of the time expressions to talk about your own job.

14

A Find pairs of statements which have the same meaning.

1 This is what I think.
2 Good morning everyone. Great to see you.
3 Let's come back to that in fifteen minutes.
4 I'm sorry I'm late.
5 Here are the results of the test.
6 You're right about that.

A I suggest we take a short break.
B I apologize for being late.
C Let me present the test results.
D Let me give you my thoughts on this.
E I agree with you.
F Welcome to our meeting today.

Which sentences do you find easier to understand?

B Match the phrases with their function in a meeting. Then brainstorm what else you can say at these points during a meeting.

1 welcoming everyone
2 dealing with technology
3 asking for feedback
4 giving an opinion
5 asking if everyone agrees
6 encouraging someone to speak
7 focusing the discussion
8 changing the subject
9 suggesting a break
10 closing the meeting

A Can you dial in again?
B We haven't heard from Jens yet.
C If you ask me, …
D Hello everyone. Thank you for being on time.
E Does anyone need a cup of coffee?
F Can we stick to the agenda, please?
G So, do we all agree on that?
H OK, so let me sum up what we've agreed.
I I'd like to hear everyone's opinion on this, please.
J Can we come back to that later?

15

A **36**)) Listen to the end of a web meeting. Peter asks the two participants from Brazil, Gustavo and Ana, a question. What is the question and how do they answer?

B About half an hour after the meeting, Gustavo sends an email to Victoria. Read his email and the comments she sends back to him. What do you think went wrong at the meeting?

Dear Gustavo

You'll find my answers in red below.

bw Vicky

Victoria,

During the meeting earlier you talked about the documents for the DTBR project. Please check if these are the documents Ana and I should send.

Default Concept   *I think you mean the technical documentation, right? Yes, please send.*

User Document   *No need to send, Peter sent you this excel file.*

Training Document   *Peter sent you this.*

You can find examples of each document in the attachments.

Is this correct?

Gustavo

16 The British have a reputation for being indirect. Look at some examples of what they might say. Do you understand what the phrases in blue mean? Add in your interpretation, then look at **File 22** → page 76 to see if you were right.

What the British say	What you understand
By the way, I was wondering if you'd had a chance to do that report?	
Please think about this again before you start.	
It's probably my fault.	

17 **A** Communication style is a personal choice, but in general, people from eastern cultures prefer indirect communication and people from most western cultures prefer a more direct approach. Read a short dialogue and then answer the questions.

Ms Swift	I know it's very soon, but can you finish the report by Friday? The delegation from New York is arriving on Saturday and it would be great to have it before our meeting.
Mr Nguyen	I'll do my best.
Ms Swift	Excellent. That will be a great help. Could you come into the office on Saturday afternoon so that we can discuss it with them?
Mr Nguyen	Yes, but it might be difficult.
Ms Swift	Good. Thank you.
Mr Nguyen	Saturday is my son's fifth birthday.
Ms Swift	I can't believe he's five already! I hope he has a lovely party.
Mr Nguyen	Thank you. That's very kind of you.

1 Does Ms Swift expect to discuss the report with the visitors and Mr Nguyen on Saturday?
2 Do you think Mr Nguyen hands in the report and comes to the office on Saturday?

B Look back at what Mr Nguyen said and decide what he meant. Compare your ideas with an interpretation in **File 23** → page 76. If you have ever had an experience like this, describe what happened.

> **Film 3** 🎬 You can watch the film in which three people talk about communication styles in their country. Before you watch, turn to the exercises on page 100.

18 One way to sound less direct in conversation is to use *not* with a positive word, e.g. *bad = not good*. We can also add words like *very, so, quite, a bit, totally* to soften the comment, e.g. *that's not so good.* Reformulate these sentences to make them sound more positive using the words in brackets.

> It's going to be difficult to solve that problem.

> It's not going to be easy to solve that problem.

1 The project was managed badly. (well)
2 The sales results were disappointing. (encouraging)
3 The meeting was a disaster. (successful)
4 The figures were wrong. (correct)
5 The food in the canteen is terrible. (tasty)

19 **A** Telling someone what to do directly may sound rude in many cultures. Brainstorm the best way to make this order sound more like a request.

Come to my office at 2 pm. (*team leader to team member*)

B The question "Do you understand?" can be problematic in some cultures. It is difficult to say you aren't sure without seeming stupid. How can you check that the teams understand what to do in a less direct way?

20

A How do you like to work? Choose your preferences from this list. Why do you like working that way?

direct communication	indirect communication
fixed rules	flexible rules
punctuality	flexible attitude to time
clear, brief instructions	diplomatic instructions
honest discussion	group harmony
team decides	team leader decides
open criticism	no criticism

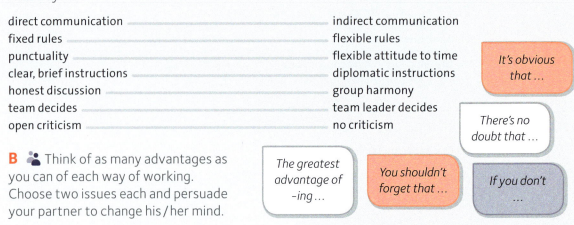

It's obvious that …

There's no doubt that …

B Think of as many advantages as you can of each way of working. Choose two issues each and persuade your partner to change his / her mind.

The greatest advantage of -ing …

You shouldn't forget that …

If you don't …

21

Read these ideas from a forum discussion on teamwork. What matches your own experience?

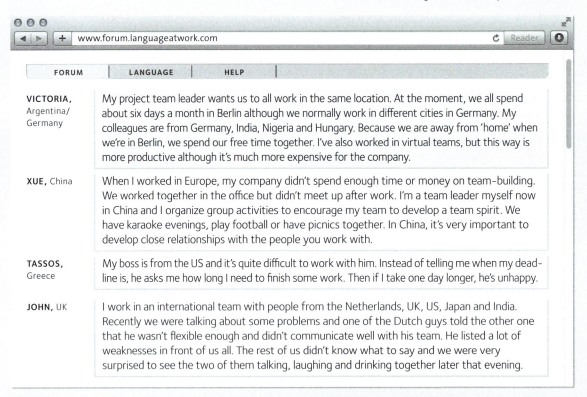

www.forum.languageatwork.com

| FORUM | LANGUAGE | HELP |

VICTORIA, Argentina/Germany
My project team leader wants us to all work in the same location. At the moment, we all spend about six days a month in Berlin although we normally work in different cities in Germany. My colleagues are from Germany, India, Nigeria and Hungary. Because we are away from 'home' when we're in Berlin, we spend our free time together. I've also worked in virtual teams, but this way is more productive although it's much more expensive for the company.

XUE, China
When I worked in Europe, my company didn't spend enough time or money on team-building. We worked together in the office but didn't meet up after work. I'm a team leader myself now in China and I organize group activities to encourage my team to develop a team spirit. We have karaoke evenings, play football or have picnics together. In China, it's very important to develop close relationships with the people you work with.

TASSOS, Greece
My boss is from the US and it's quite difficult to work with him. Instead of telling me when my deadline is, he asks me how long I need to finish some work. Then if I take one day longer, he's unhappy.

JOHN, UK
I work in an international team with people from the Netherlands, UK, US, Japan and India. Recently we were talking about some problems and one of the Dutch guys told the other one that he wasn't flexible enough and didn't communicate well with his team. He listed a lot of weaknesses in front of us all. The rest of us didn't know what to say and we were very surprised to see the two of them talking, laughing and drinking together later that evening.

22

Project Work

It is your task to lead a new project team which will work together for eight months. In addition to team members from your own office, colleagues from India, Brazil, Finland and China are in the team. Consider what you have discussed in this unit so far and think about these questions:

1. What problems might there be in working with such a mixed group?
2. What could you do to avoid or minimize them?
3. How could you change your own way of working to make it easier for the international team members?

Present your ideas to the head of your department.

Use an example from your own company if you like.

23

Useful language

Complete these sentences with a suitable word.

1   Can we _____ a time for a telephone conference?

2   Sure. Are you _____ on Friday morning?

3   Yes, that _____ for me.

4   I'm really sorry but I'll have to _____ the meeting.

5   Could we _____ for tomorrow?

24

Useful language

A Look at your calendar (private and work) for the next seven days. Have you made arrangements for these times? Write sentences about yourself.

a   (this evening) I'm going to yoga this evening. / I'm not doing anything this evening.

b   (Friday morning) _____

c   (Tuesday afternoon) _____

d   (Saturday evening) _____

e   (Wednesday morning) _____

B 👥 With a partner, make two appointments – one at work and one after work. Write down what you are doing and when.

25

Listening: being direct and indirect

37))) If you are at a meeting with people from an indirect culture, what would you understand if someone says:

1   That's a very interesting point of view.

2   I don't know a lot about this, but ...

3   Can we move on to the next topic?

Listen to the opinion of an intercultural trainer. Is her interpretation similar to yours?

26

Grammar: *when* or *if*?

Complete the sentences with *when* or *if*. There is only one correct answer.

1   _____ the team meets for the first time, it's a good idea to have a meal in a restaurant together.

2   I'm planning to see Gustavo _____ I visit the Brazilian office next month.

3   Please call me _____ you have any questions about the meeting.

4   We'll present the software to the users next week, _____ they're available.

5   I'll call you _____ I arrive at the hotel.

> **Before the next class** Think about yourself as a consumer. Make a list of what you expect when you buy a product or a service.

> **For the next unit** Take a good look at your company's website and make a note of what you like about it and any improvements you would suggest.

1

A Look at the photos. Do they show a product, a service or both?

B Choose from the expressions below to describe each product or service in the photos. Can you add any more descriptions of your own?

appliance • device • equipment • machine • product • service • software • solution • structure	attractive • compact • convenient • customizable • easy-to-use • economical • environmentally-friendly • flexible • highly-specialized • innovative • user-friendly • well-designed

C Imagine you work for a company which sells one of these products or services. Tell a potential customer what you offer. Add your own ideas.

We ...	offer a(n) provide a(n)	convenient economical effective innovative practical quick	way to ...	achieve ... create ... improve ... increase ... prevent ... reduce ...

2

A **38**)) Listen to Lukáš talking about his company What does his company do? What do they offer their customers?

> *Does your company work B2B (business to business) or B2C (business to client)?*

B Compare your company with Ice Factory. What product or service does your company sell? Who are your customers? Use the phrases here and in **1** to help you.

Similarities
We are/do ... too.
We aren't/don't ..., either.

Differences
Our company is completely different. We ...
There's no comparison. Our clients ...

3

A 👥 Work with a partner. Partner A is a private customer and wants to buy a washing machine. Partner B is a business customer and wants to buy a CNC* machine for the factory production line. Rank customer expectations from 1 (most important) to 8 (least important).

- ◯ good value for money
- ◯ free delivery of goods to your door
- ◯ excellent references from satisfied customers
- ◯ high quality goods/services
- ◯ reliable after-sales service

- ◯ salespeople with relevant know-how
- ◯ understanding of legal and environmental standards
- ◯ innovative solutions to customers' problems

* computer numerical control

B Who are your company's customers? What do you think their priorities are?

4

A Consumer electronics is big business. Look at the infographic below showing how often certain items are replaced and why. How often do you replace the items mentioned?

Why do people replace devices?

40% they have upgraded to a new device

20% the devices don't work

40% they don't need or use them

TV sets are replaced every 5–7 years.
PCs, tablets, etc. are replaced every 3–4 years.
Smartphones are replaced every 1–3 years.
The average company replaces electronic equipment every 3 years.

B 👥 What happens to the old devices? What do companies do with their old equipment? Read the short text below and then discuss the questions with a partner.

Worldwide, there are about 50 million tons of electronic waste every year. In the EU, which has stricter controls than other regions, only about 25 % of e-waste is recycled.

a How often does your company replace its electronic equipment?
b How does your company deal with e-waste?
c What happens to the company data on old equipment?
d Why is it necessary to find a solution to the problem of unwanted equipment?

5

Language Focus: talking about rules, laws and standards

a must / have to = it's necessary
Must suggests that the speaker thinks something is necessary.
Have to suggests that the speaker is following a rule or that someone else has said something is necessary.
Have to can be used in the present, the past and the future, e. g. *have to; had to; will have to.*
Must is only used in the present and is replaced by a form of *have to* in the other tenses.

b mustn't = not allowed, forbidden

c don't / doesn't have to = not necessary

Now complete the sentences.

1 According to EU law, all companies _____ [1] manage their electronic waste in a responsible way.
2 Companies _____ [2] throw employee data away; it _____ [3] be removed from old electronic devices. This is the law.
3 All businesses _____ [4] use the services of an e-waste recycling company in order to prove they have high environmental standards, and they _____ [5] work with a company which is not registered with the Environment Agency.
4 A business _____ [6] recycle its old equipment, but it _____ [7] store it securely.

6

A ASECCA is a UK company which recycles e-waste. Match what the people are looking for with the descriptions on ASECCA's website.

> *I'm looking for a job.*

> *We don't know what to do with our e-waste.*

> *At our company, we're very worried about security.*

> *How does the service work?*

If electronic recycling is new to you or your organization, we can help. We aim to make your recycling process as simple as possible.	Our people are at the heart of everything we do. We welcome all applications. For further information, please email our HR department.
Open an account with a member of our team – a 10 minute process where we keep the demands on your time to an absolute minimum.	We use the best resources in the world to guarantee the sensitive data on your mobile phone is destroyed.

B As a company website is often the first point of contact with a company, what other information and features are important to include there?

A website should always have ...

A website has to ...

7

One option to find out more about what a company does is to email them. Read the email to ASECCA and answer the questions.

1 What is the purpose of the email?

2 Does the email include all of the elements below? Keep in mind who the email has been sent to.

    a opening salutation   d request for action
    b introduction   e closing sentence
    c reason for writing   f closing salutation

3 How would you write such an email? Discuss with a partner.

> *Have you ever seen enquiries sent to your company? Are they like this one?*

Date: 22.06.20-- 10:16:05 BST
From: m.hunter@alconsult.co.uk
To: info@asecca.co.uk
Subject: Enquiry

ASECCA has been recommended to us by a business partner. We are a financial consulting company and deal with a lot of very sensitive client data so the security aspects of your service are of particular interest to us.

As we are also based in Lancaster, I would like to arrange a meeting to discuss the whole process. Please let me know when this would be convenient.

We are looking forward to hearing from you soon.

Best regards

Marcus Hunter

Head of IT

Alconsult Ltd

8

A **39)))** Many potential customers prefer to speak to a sales executive before they decide to place an order with ASECCA. Listen to a telephone conversation between an account manager and a new customer. What does the customer want to know?

B When you want to find out more about a product or service, how do you get the information?

9

A What does a company have to do to keep you as a customer? Use the points below and your own ideas to make a short questionnaire. Then interview the rest of the class to find out what they think.

cool image • ethical business behaviour • good service • good value for money • quality of products • special offers

B More and more people share their experiences on social networks. How much do good or bad reviews influence you?

10

A A "good customer experience" may not mean the same thing to everyone or to people from all cultures. Read about some possible differences.

Customer experience and culture

Companies have to develop effective strategies for customer care because any negative experience can be tweeted around the world and have a bad effect on the company's image. As companies go global, they must learn what customers in different countries expect, and train their staff to connect with them. Certain expectations are universal, but not all. This list of questions just begins to show what differences there can be.

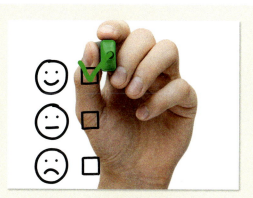

1 Do you want your customer service agent (CSA) to become your best friend for the few minutes they need to solve your problem?
2 Would you expect to use first names with a CSA?
3 "The customer is always right." Is this how you want to be treated?
4 How important is "service with a smile" to you? Is friendly service enough?
5 How would you react if an agent suggested that you had made a mistake?
6 How quickly do you expect an answer?
7 Do you ask for help with every little problem, or only if something serious happens?
8 As a customer, do you see the agent as your equal, as a "colleague" who solves the problem with you and not for you?
9 Is the solution to a problem enough or do you expect an explanation as well?
10 Is it OK to get angry?

Now decide what you would prefer if you were **a** the customer or **b** the customer service agent.

B As the article says, there are some general rules about good customer care. Complete these rules with the right verb. Add some of your own ideas to the list.

accept • ask • deal • keep • listen • revise • show • train • treat

Rules of effective customer care

1 _____ your staff well so they have the know-how to answer customers' questions.

2 _____ promises so that your customers are not disappointed.

3 You want satisfied customers so if something goes wrong, _____ with their complaints quickly. _____ customers fairly.

4 _____ to your customers and _____ them that they are important by developing a personal relationship with them.

5 _____ your customers for feedback and _____ criticism. _____ your strategy if necessary.

11 **Language Focus: talking about feelings and opinions**

Look at the sentences below.

The book is boring. (the book causes the feeling/opinion)

I was bored when I read the book. (this was the effect on me)

cause	convincing	interesting	satisfying	surprising
effect	convinced	interested	satisfied	surprised

Choose the correct form of the adjective in the following sentences.

1 The speaker just read from his notes so the talk was very _____ (boring/bored).
2 Although the company has a very good reputation, I was _____ (disappointing/disappointed) with the service.
3 I was so _____ (annoying/annoyed) when the machine broke down again.
4 The reason she gave for the delay was not very _____ (convincing/convinced).
5 I'm very _____ (interesting/interested) in seeing the new product.

12 **A** 👥 What should or shouldn't you say to customers? For each of these examples, discuss with a partner why it's not a good idea and then suggest what you could say instead.

1 You're wrong.
2 I've never done this before.
3 No one has ever asked me that before.
4 That's not my job.
5 Please calm down.

B Compare your ideas with suggestions from a customer service blog.
Partner A → **File 24**, page 77.   Partner B → **File 25**, page 79.

13 **A** If a customer complains, there are three steps you can take to deal with it.

Step 1: Show that you are listening.
Step 2: Show that you understand the customer's frustration.
Step 3: Offer a solution or, at least, show that you will deal with the problem.

Match these expressions with the three steps.

What seems to be the problem? .... ◯   I'm very sorry that this has happened. .... ◯
I'm sure I can help you to sort this out. .... ◯   Let me see what I can do. .... ◯
Can you explain exactly what the problem is? ..... ◯   So you're saying ...? .... ◯
Can I get back to you this afternoon? .... ◯   How annoying! .... ◯
I do apologize on behalf of the company. .... ◯

B Add more ideas of your own.

14 **A** When was the last time you complained about a faulty product or bad service (privately or professionally)? Describe why you complained and what happened. Were you satisfied with the result?

B 👥 Work with a partner. Choose one of your experiences from **A** and follow the instructions for the role-play.
Partner A → **File 26**, page 73.   Partner B → **File 27**, page 79.

15

A Read what people say about working with native English speakers. Have you ever had similar experiences?

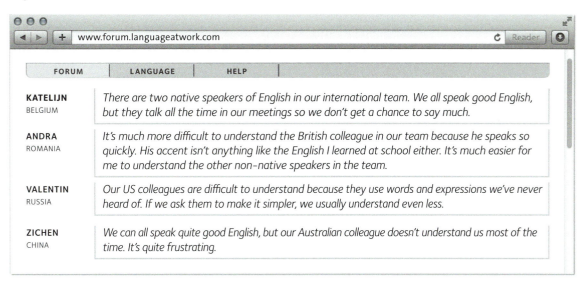

KATELIJN BELGIUM	*There are two native speakers of English in our international team. We all speak good English, but they talk all the time in our meetings so we don't get a chance to say much.*
ANDRA ROMANIA	*It's much more difficult to understand the British colleague in our team because he speaks so quickly. His accent isn't anything like the English I learned at school either. It's much easier for me to understand the other non-native speakers in the team.*
VALENTIN RUSSIA	*Our US colleagues are difficult to understand because they use words and expressions we've never heard of. If we ask them to make it simpler, we usually understand even less.*
ZICHEN CHINA	*We can all speak quite good English, but our Australian colleague doesn't understand us most of the time. It's quite frustrating.*

B What differences do you notice in the way you speak when you use English compared to when you speak your native language?

16

A Have you ever spoken to people from English-speaking countries? How easy or difficult were they to understand?

B 40)) Listen to speakers from four of these places. Can you identify where they are from by their accents? Number the places as you listen. Who do you find the easiest and the most difficult to understand?

Australasia ◯   Britain ◯   India ◯   Ireland ◯   North America ◯   South Africa ◯

C Turn to page 91 and read what the speakers say while you listen. What do you notice about their pronunciation?

17

A When native speakers want to make their language simpler, they often do it this way: "I'll collect you from your hotel tomorrow morning" becomes "I'll pick you up from your hotel tomorrow morning". Which sentence do you think is easier to understand?

B Multi-word verbs like the ones below are a typical feature of native-speaker English. Which ones are correct?

1 Please fill in/fill up the form.
2 I'm looking after/looking for the meeting room.
3 I hope I can get my message across/get my message through.

C Rewrite these sentences by replacing the underlined verb with a multi-word verb.

1 Let's <u>continue</u> working after lunch.
2 Do you want to <u>postpone</u> our meeting until 3 pm?
3 This problem <u>requires</u> a quick solution.
4 I'll try to <u>connect</u> you to the HR Manager.
5 I've <u>cancelled</u> my visit to the factory.
6 What's <u>happening</u> outside?

call (2x) ● carry ● go ● put ● put

for ● off (2x) ● on (2x) ● through

18 Read the short text below and then answer the questions.

A man dies shortly after renting a car and the agency refuses to let the family pay the fees for the rental. It's the stuff of dreams! Yet, in this case, it's real, and it's exactly the kind of customer service we all wish for. But even if this behaviour is unusual, as customers we increasingly expect more from service providers. 90 % of us use social media to describe our experiences of a company and we expect companies to listen; 34 % of us want to get a reply to our queries on Twitter or Facebook within 15 minutes of posting them. And the 60 % of companies who don't respond via social media are losing money. The idea that you have to "spend money to make money" is understood when a product is produced or marketed, but often not in after-sales care. This takes us back to the car rental agency: what would you have done in their position?

1 What did the car rental agency do?

2 What do consumers expect from companies nowadays regarding customer service?

3 What could be the reason for a company's poor customer service?

19 **A** Companies claim many things. Complete these sentences from different companies with the verbs below.

advise ● aim ● ensure ● guarantee ● support ● welcome

1 _____ to Europe's number one household appliance manufacturer.

2 We _____ delivery within 24 hours or you get your money back.

3 Our team of consultants can _____ you on the best financial products for your needs.

4 We _____ that the needs of our customers come first.

5 Wherever our customers are located, we _____ to provide the best possible service.

6 We _____ a wide range of educational and environmental projects.

B Use some of the verbs to describe what your company offers its customers.

C Think of a company you've recently done business with. What did you expect as a customer? What "promises" are important or less important to you?

20 👥 **Project Work**

1 Work with a partner. Each of you choose a company website you know well, either your own company's website or one you use as a customer. If possible, choose different companies and include one service company, such as your phone provider.

2 Find out what options are given to customers to contact the company. Does the company have an email address or an online contact form? Do they use call centres? Do they have a social media presence? Do they use more traditional media?

3 Collect your ideas. Do you think the various contact options are useful? If you've used them, were you happy with the service? Which options could be improved?

4 Using your ideas, now write a list of dos and don'ts for a company's contact options for its customers. Keep the list short (6–8 items) and either make it for your own company or another company of your choice.

21 Useful language

A Match the sentence halves.

1 Our client base is	A environmentally-friendly.
2 Most of our work is	B software for the chemical industry.
3 We are a leading manufacturer	C in the B2B sector.
4 We aim to make our products	D growing all the time.
5 Our products are guaranteed to be	E of parts for the automotive industry.
6 We develop highly-specialized	F as economical as possible.

B Now rewrite them to make true sentences about your company.

---

22 Useful language

A **41**))) Listen and complete the information below.

_____ % of customer service contacts are on the phone. 85 % are _____ with this experience. 72 % of customers think it takes too long to _____ _____ _____ . 84 % of customers get _____ because agents can't find their customer information quickly. _____ customers tell 5 people about their experience. Dissatisfied customers tell _____ people about their experience. 89 % of dissatisfied customers _____ _____ _____ with the company.

B Write some advice for companies based on the information above.

1 You should _____

2 You mustn't _____

3 You don't have to _____

4 You shouldn't _____

5 You have to _____

---

23 Grammar: must / have to

Complete these sentences with a form of *must* or *have to*.

1 My new client has phoned twice already. I'll _____ go to see him next week.
2 All toys made in the EU _____ carry the CE marking.
3 You _____ stay until 4pm today if you don't want to. I'll answer your phone.
4 The company _____ recall one of their products because there was a safety problem.

---

24 Grammar: cause or effect?

Choose the correct word in each sentence.

1 I was very **frustrated/frustrating** by the poor customer service I experienced.
2 We all came out of the meeting totally **confused/confusing**. No one knows what we have to do next.
3 The speaker was very **amused/amusing**, but the information he gave us wasn't very useful.
4 My new job is quite **challenged/challenging** and that's why I enjoy it.

Before the next class Find out how important trade fairs are for your company. Does the company exhibit at trade fairs? Do employees attend them? Share what you have found out in class.

For the next unit Check the meaning of the term *false friends*. Make a list of some common false friends in English and your own language. Bring the list to class.

08 Preparing for a trade fair

1

A How can a company attract customers? Make a list of the advantages and disadvantages of each method.

article/review in trade journal • freebies • print advert • social media • trade fair stand • TV advert

> A YouTube™ video can show customers how to use products.

> An article in a trade journal can seem more serious than an advertisement.

> Social media tools are free but it takes a lot of staff time to keep information up to date.

B **42))** Listen to a conversation about the importance of trade fairs and answer the questions.

1 Why does Maria think it is a good idea to take part in a trade fair?
2 Why is Steve not so sure that it makes good business sense?

C Listen again and complete the sentences below. Then give your own opinion of trade fairs. Use the expressions to help you.

> How important are trade fairs to your company?

1 Personally, I think

2 If you ask me,

3 I may be wrong, but

4 As far as I know,

5 There's no doubt that

2

A Match the words and phrases which have a similar meaning.

1 free samples	A fair grounds
2 stand	B leaflets
3 brochures	C venue
4 stand personnel	D freebies
5 location	E booth staff
6 exhibition hall	F booth

B With a partner, think about the ways in which products can be presented at a trade fair. Which options do you think work well? Which are less effective or important?

3

A 43))) Maria's company manufactures medical equipment. They are planning to exhibit at a trade fair. The events team has called a meeting to discuss the fair. Which booth do they choose and why?

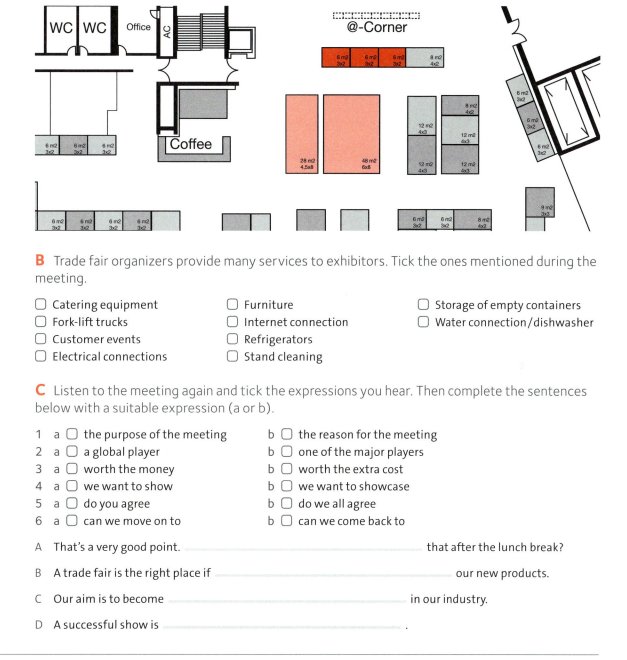

B Trade fair organizers provide many services to exhibitors. Tick the ones mentioned during the meeting.

- ☐ Catering equipment
- ☐ Fork-lift trucks
- ☐ Customer events
- ☐ Electrical connections
- ☐ Furniture
- ☐ Internet connection
- ☐ Refrigerators
- ☐ Stand cleaning
- ☐ Storage of empty containers
- ☐ Water connection/dishwasher

C Listen to the meeting again and tick the expressions you hear. Then complete the sentences below with a suitable expression (a or b).

1 a ☐ the purpose of the meeting   b ☐ the reason for the meeting
2 a ☐ a global player   b ☐ one of the major players
3 a ☐ worth the money   b ☐ worth the extra cost
4 a ☐ we want to show   b ☐ we want to showcase
5 a ☐ do you agree   b ☐ do we all agree
6 a ☐ can we move on to   b ☐ can we come back to

A   That's a very good point. _____ that after the lunch break?

B   A trade fair is the right place if _____ our new products.

C   Our aim is to become _____ in our industry.

D   A successful show is _____ .

4

Language Focus: giving your opinion
We often introduce our opinion with a short phrase to make it seem less direct. The same applies when you agree and especially if you disagree with someone.

A   Giving your opinion:
1   Personally, I think …
2   In my experience …
3   I believe it/that …

B   Agreeing with an opinion:
1   I'd go along with that.
2   I agree with you completely.
3   That's just what I was thinking.

C   Disagreeing with an opinion:
1   I'm sorry to disagree with you, but …
2   Yes, but don't you think …?
3   I'm not so sure about that.

Now rewrite the short dialogue below so it is less direct. Use the phrases above or others that you know.
A: We should use our own construction company to build our booth.
B: No. It makes more sense to use the construction team offered by the fair organizers.
C: Yes.

5 Exhibitors book booth space and services from a trade fair organizer, but what other preparations are necessary before a fair? Make a note of your ideas based on what you know or think your company does.

for company staff	for customers

6 **A** Read this email from Maria's colleague Julia. Does it match the ideas you had in **5**?

From	julia.miles@medapp.com
To	groupsales@apexhotel.com
Subject	Block booking 14.11.–18.11.15

Dear Mr Lalani,

Further to our conversation this morning, I would like to confirm the block booking made for the period 14.11.-18.11.15. Please charge our company account (details below).

Please note that only room charges may be charged to the account. Hotel guests will pay for any extra costs such as mini-bar purchases themselves.

Please send me a group sales contract which includes the following information:

rate per room

confirmation that up to five additional rooms can be booked at group discount rate

confirmation that parking (if required) is included in the room rate

confirmation of priority check-in and check-out

details of the hotel cancellation policy

B Find phrases in the email which do the following.

1 refer to previous communication

2 state the reason for writing

3 give instructions

4 give information

5 request something

7 **A** Maria has drafted an invitation to send to customers before the Life Science trade fair. Read it and underline the phrases used for the purposes mentioned in **6B**. What differences do you notice?

Dear ...

Thank you for requesting complimentary tickets for this year's Life Science trade fair. You will find them in the attachment along with a copy of the floor plan of the exhibition halls.

We look forward to welcoming you to booth A24 in Hall 1 to see our brand new DA 16 dialysis machine. Our sales staff are looking forward to demonstrating our products and answering any questions you may have.

As one of our most valued customers, we would like to invite you to a wine and cheese reception followed by a networking event. Please make a note of the time and place: Booth A24, November 15th at 6pm. Please bring your business card along with you to take part in our in-booth tombola. There are great prizes to be won!

If you would like to make a personal appointment with one of our staff on any of the fair days, please contact me and I will make the arrangements.

We are looking forward to seeing you again at Life Science.

B What kind of events does your company organize for customers?
Write an invitation and compare it with a partner.

8

A **44))** Messe Basel, a trade fair organizer, provides an online logistics tool for arranging deliveries. Listen to the logistics manager explaining the process, and put the steps into the right order. The first and last have been done for you.

a ◯ The next step is the arrival of your forwarding agent at the checkpoint.
b ◯ After that, the lorry can drive to the delivery zone.
c ◯ Now you can commission your forwarding agent.
d (**1**) The first step is to log on to our logistics tool.
e ◯ Then our agent transports the stand construction material to the booth.
f ◯ Then you receive a registration confirmation.
g ◯ At this point, our official forwarding agent unloads the cargo.
h (**8**) Finally, the forwarder transports the products to the booth.

forwarding agent = freight forwarder 🔍

B Read some frequently asked questions (FAQs) about the logistics process at Messe Basel. How would you answer them? If you are not sure, listen again.

Do you have experience of this aspect of trade fair preparation? 🏢

Frequently Asked Questions

MESSE BASEL

1 Can I log on to the logistics tool free of charge?

2 Can my forwarding agent unload the stand construction material in the delivery zone and take it to the booth space?

3 How long is the time limit for unloading in the delivery zone?

9

A **45))** What can go wrong during the logistics process? Listen to a call to the logistics helpline and decide which of the statements are true (T) or false (F).

1 ◯ Julia has made a mistake.
2 ◯ The forwarding agent has had an accident.
3 ◯ The driver can get a new delivery pass at the checkpoint.
4 ◯ The driver can go straight through to the delivery zone.
5 ◯ The helpline agent tells Julia that the lorry will be unloaded today.
6 ◯ Julia isn't worried.

B Describe a process which is part of your work. Use the sequencing expressions in **8** to show the steps. What can go wrong and how can you solve the problem?

10

A Things may go wrong and there are always last-minute jobs to do before a trade fair starts. Put these statements into the correct categories.

A pointing out a problem   **B** requesting help   **C** apologizing   **D** promising to help

1 ◯ I'll sort this out for you.
2 ◯ I'm afraid we're going to miss the deadline.
3 ◯ We're having trouble with our internet connection.
4 ◯ I'm sorry about the inconvenience.
5 ◯ I'll make sure someone comes to the booth.
6 ◯ What can we do about it?
7 ◯ I think there's something wrong with the cable.
8 ◯ Don't worry, we can do that by tomorrow morning.

B It is the day before the fair opens and there is still work to do. Role-play the situation.
Partner A → **File** 28, page 71.   **Partner B** → **File** 29, page 79.

11

A How can you prepare to attend a trade fair abroad for the first time? What information do you need?

B Now read a short interview given by an international business consultant to promote her global awareness workshops. How many of the points you thought of in **A** does she mention?

TIPS FOR SUCCESS AT INTERNATIONAL TRADE FAIRS

Q: *Trade show expectations and rules may be totally different from host country to host country. How can companies prepare to succeed?*

Personally, I think that the best way to start is to go to a fair as a visitor to see who the other attendees are and which companies exhibit at the fair. There's no doubt that you can pick up a lot of extremely useful information this way. Exhibiting at international trade fairs means a large investment of time and money so it's really necessary to get it right.

Q: *What should companies do to overcome language barriers?*

I may be wrong, but I think that many companies, especially ones based in English-speaking countries, assume they can do all their business in English, anywhere in the world. This is a highly risky strategy. In many countries, it's absolutely vital to have booth staff who can communicate in the local language, and if this is impossible, to hire good, local interpreters and give them training about the products. It may be quite obvious, but written materials and signs at the booth should also be translated.

Q: *How can companies be sure that their products arrive at the exhibition on time?*

If you ask me, and this is especially true if you are exhibiting for the first time in a country, the best option is to use the official freight forwarder for the fair. They have experience of the location and will know how to deal with the local customs regulations and the customs officials.

Q: *How much help can a company expect from the fair organizers?*

Just like at home, international fair organizers give exhibitors a lot of help. The online registration process itself will answer many questions, but my experience shows that a little local knowledge is extremely valuable. Should we offer in-booth hospitality, for example? Exhibitors should know if visitors expect snacks and drinks when they visit the booth as this will help determine the size of booth needed. Should we hire a local stand construction company? What stand design is the most suitable? These are just a few of the questions I deal with in my workshops.

12

Language Focus: being more specific
Some adverbs are used with adjectives to answer the questions "how" or "to what extent".

How enjoyable was the event?	It was **perfectly OK**, though I didn't stay long.
Was the workshop useful?	Well, yes, it was **fairly useful**, but it could have been better.

1 Read through the interview in **11B** again and underline all the adverb/adjective combinations.
2 Make three true sentences about your job using an adverb/adjective combination in each one, e. g. **My job is extremely interesting.** Use the words below to help you.

adverb
absolutely ● completely ● extremely ●
easily ● fairly ● highly ● quite ● rather

adjective
clear ● difficult ● easy ● interesting ●
normal ● popular ● simple ● successful

13

A The consultant gives a lot of country-specific information during her workshops. Choose a country which interests you. Write down what you learn about **a** translating written materials, **b** booth construction and **c** hospitality.

Brazil → **File** 30, page 77. China → **File** 31, page 76.
Russia → **File** 32, page 75. UAE → **File** 33, page 78.
USA → **File** 34, page 79.

> *Do you do business in any of these countries? Have you ever exhibited at a trade fair there?*

B Compare what you've found out with a partner who has looked at a different country. If you can, add any further details you can based on your own experience.

14 At trade fairs you can often expect to hear people speaking many different varieties of English. What do you think are the biggest challenges to understanding each other? Think about the following points and talk about your experiences.

- vocabulary mistakes people may make
- how people pronounce English sounds

> *What nationalities do you come into contact with at work?*

15 **A** The words in the blue columns are "true friends" in these languages because they have the same meaning, but the similar-looking English word is a "false friend" because the meaning is different.

Czech	aktuálni		eventuálně	
Dutch	actueel		eventueel	
French	actuel		éventuel	
German	aktuell	actual	eventuell	eventual
Polish	aktualny		ewentualny	
Spanish	actual		eventual	
Swedish	aktuell		eventuellt	

What do the English words *actual(ly)* and *eventual(ly)* mean? Write a sentence using each one, then translate them into your own language.

B Look at these English words. Are there similar words in your own language and in any other languages you speak? Discuss whether the meanings are the same in each language.

brave ● chef ● control ● expertise ● lecture ● magazine ● realize ● sensible ● sympathetic

C Choose three of the words and make up sentences to show the meaning in English.

> *What other common false friends in English and your own language can you think of?*

16 **A** **46))** Certain sounds in English can be difficult for non-native speakers. Listen to four speakers talking about some of the problems they have.

1 Which sounds are mentioned most often?
2 Were you surprised by any of the comments? If so, why?
3 Are there any sounds in English which you find particularly difficult?

> *If you speak English to other non-native speakers, do you find speakers from some countries especially difficult to understand? Who do you find easier?*

B Think about your own language. Are there sounds in your native language which cause non-native speakers problems?

17 Preparing for a trade fair involves a lot of work. Look at the checklist below. In which order would you do them? Can you think of any other points which are missing?

> ### CHECKLIST
>
> ☐ Decide which shows to visit and the purpose of exhibiting
> ☐ Decide on budget for the fair(s)
> ☐ Get information about size of booths, position, etc.
> ☐ Decide on size and design of booth
> ☐ Apply for a stand and make first payments
> ☐ Decide who will staff your booth
> ☐ Order name badges and/or uniforms
> ☐ Plan your marketing strategy for the fair
> ☐ Order your free samples/freebies
> ☐ Book hotel rooms for staff
> ☐ Organize shipping of materials
> ☐ Send out information about the fair to customers
> ☐ Confirm all details with staff

18 **Project Work**

Have a meeting to discuss your plans for your company's exhibition stand at the next trade fair.

1   Agree on an agenda for the meeting.

2   Decide who is going to chair the meeting, act as timekeeper and write the minutes.

3   Then discuss the questions below.
   a   Is it better to buy or rent a stand? What impact does this decision have?
   b   What is the best location for a stand in an exhibition hall?
   c   What are the advantages and disadvantages of island or inline spaces?
   d   What makes a stand attractive to visitors?
   e   How can a stand present the image of a company?
   f   What booth layout invites visitors to enter?
   g   How much multimedia is a good idea?
   h   What can visitors do in the booth?
   i   Is it necessary to hire a booth design company?

4   Note down the decisions you have made and what points are still open.

> **Film 4** 🎬 If you want to see what goes on backstage at a trade fair, you can watch the preparations for Baselworld. Before you watch, turn to the exercises on page 104.

19

Grammar: adverb/adjective combinations

Choose one of the most suitable adjectives below to complete each sentence. Not all of them are needed.

annoying • clean • complex • dirty • easy • essential • expected • popular • unexpected • unpopular • useless • wonderful

1   After the cleaning staff had left, our stand was still quite _____ so I contacted the hall manager.

2   It's absolutely _____ to register in good time if you want to book an island booth.

3   Our products are highly _____ so our customers need to understand how they work.

4   It's especially _____ if you plan everything very carefully and then something

    totally _____ happens.

5   Our special events are extremely _____ with visitors to the fair.

20

Listening for specific information

A 47)) Listen to two conversations between Meera and two members of staff at the trade fair in Basel. Then answer the questions.

1   Who does Meera know better?   a ☐ Marcin   b ☐ Marcus
2   She makes two requests. Which request is she not sure will be possible?
    a ☐ bringing the cases to the stand
    b ☐ getting access to the booth early
3   Of the two men, who is more senior?   a ☐ Marcin   b ☐ Marcus

B Listen to the conversations again. Think about your answers in **A**. Why did you answer as you did? Listen in particular to the greetings and how Meera phrases her requests.

21

Useful language

Complete these sentences with a suitable phrase.

but don't you think • I think • I agree • in my experience • I understand your point, but to me • that's just what I was thinking

Anna   _____[1] we should limit the number of fairs we visit to the two most important ones.

Susanne   _____[2] we risk annoying customers who are used to seeing us at the smaller, regional fairs too?

Anna   Yes, _____[3] this is a case of cost efficiency: we need to attract a lot of customers if we invest a lot of money in a fair.

Becca   _____[4] with Anna. _____[5], we spend most of the day explaining what we do to people who aren't interested. Maybe we could send free tickets to the customers you were talking about, Susanne.

Susanne   Yes, _____[6] !

> **Looking back** Look back through the book and find the topics which are most useful to you in your own work. Can you say or write what you want to in these situations?

> **Looking forward** What are your goals for the next course? Think about what you want to learn next.

Files

Unit 01 Exercise 4

You are going to dictate the following parts of three conversations to your partner and write what your partner dictates to you. You start with conversation 1.

When you have finished all three dialogues, compare what you have written with your partner's file.

Conversation 1

A Good morning, I'm Anna Müller. Could you let Mr Dekker know I'm here?

B _____

A Yes, of course. I'm the new marketing assistant.

B _____

Conversation 2

A _____

B Oh, hello Anna. Nice to meet you. I'm Marco Rossi, but please call me Marco.

A _____

B Let's go next door so I can introduce you to a few people.

Conversation 3

A I'd like to start today by introducing Anna Müller to you. She's our new marketing assistant.

B _____

Unit 02 Exercise 4

	Your company	**Partner's company**
Name of company	Penta-Electric	
Location(s)	head office in Basel, Switzerland; another office and workshop in Germany	
Key dates	founded 1993; German office opened 1996; new workshop opened 2013	
Number of employees	138	
Main products/services	the design, development and installation of automated systems for the chemical, pharmaceutical, biotechnology and paper industries	
Known for	high quality; being one of the most innovative companies in the region	

Unit 02 Exercise 14

You are the supplier. You want to find out about more about the potential customer and his/her position in the company. You want to use the opportunity to get as much information about the company as possible.

Unit 02 Exercise 14

You are on your way to a trade fair. You get into conversation with the person sitting next to you, who is also on a business trip. Find out more about what they do and where they work.

Unit 03 Exercise 2

Read the text and complete the table below.

> **Cristian**
>
> I come from Indonesia and have worked there as well as in Germany. Now I'm working in Den Haag in the Netherlands. In Germany and the Netherlands, it is easier to make small talk with the boss because we work in the same area. In Indonesia, bosses usually have separate offices.
>
> In the Netherlands it's unusual to socialize with co-workers outside the office. In my opinion it is even less common here than in Germany. In Indonesia, on the other hand, colleagues often spend time together after work – they have dinner together or go to the cinema.
>
> People in Germany and the Netherlands often prefer to separate their work from their private life. Here I have a colleague who doesn't talk about his private life at all to any of his colleagues, not even to say where he's going on holiday!
>
> When colleagues do socialize in the Netherlands, it's usually at events organized by the company. Even then, some colleagues try to avoid going if they can.
>
> I think one reason why Indonesians spend more free time with colleagues is that they tend to worry about what other people think of them. They try to please other people. So, for example, they go to company events to please their boss.

Read the text and complete the sentences.	In Germany and the Netherlands …
	In Indonesia …
What does Cristian say about the separation of work and private life?	

Unit 03 Exercise 14

You are going to talk to your partners about what you did last weekend. You start the conversation. In your culture, it is normal to interrupt other people while they are talking to show that you are interested in the conversation. Do this as often as you can.

Unit 08 Exercise 10

You have just arrived at your company's booth to make sure everything is ready for the first day of the trade fair. You were in a traffic jam so you arrived later than planned, and the exhibition hall is closing in half an hour. You notice that the information desk at the front of the booth is much too high. The stand construction team has packed up their tools and is getting ready to leave. Speak to the head of the stand construction team.

Unit 01 Exercise 4

You are going to dictate the following parts of three conversations to your partner and write what your partner dictates to you. Your partner will start with conversation 1.

When you have finished all three dialogues, compare what you have written with your partner's file.

Conversation 1

A _____

B   Certainly. Can I tell him what your visit is about?

A _____

B   Well, welcome to ITC! Please take a seat while I give him a call.

Conversation 2

A   May I introduce myself? My name's Anna Müller. I'm the new marketing assistant.

B _____

A   Hi, Marco. Nice to meet you, too.

B _____

Conversation 3

A _____

B   Thanks Mr Dekker. Good morning everyone. It's great to be here. I'm looking forward to getting to know you all.

Unit 02 Exercise 4

	Your company	Partner's company
Name of company	Malheur Brewery (old name = Sun Brewery)	
Location(s)	village of Buggenhour in Flanders, Belgium	
Key dates	founded 1839; changed name to Malheur in 1997; won title of best dark beer in the world in 2013	
Number of employees	16	
Main products/services	produces specialist beers	
Known for	combining tradtion with modern developments in brewing technology; its beer, especially its dark beer (has won prizes)	

Unit 02 Exercise 14

You are visiting a potential new supplier but are not yet sure whether you want to do business with the company. Try to find out as much as you can without giving too much information about your own company.

Unit 02 Exercise 14

It's your regular informal departmental meeting and everyone is giving an update on the status of their projects. You have only just started a new project so you don't have much to report so far. You are very interested in hearing about the other projects and ask a lot of questions.

Unit 03 Exercise 2

Read the text and complete the table below.

> **Diego**
>
> I come from Ecuador and have worked there as well as in Belgium and Germany. Now I'm working in Adelaide, Australia. My experience is that in Germany and Belgium people talk less about personal issues at work than somewhere like Ecuador or Australia. I was really surprised that Aussies are so open-minded in this respect as I thought they would be more like the Europeans I met.
>
> In Ecuador, it's very common to mix work and private life. Co-workers often spend a lot of time together, sometimes becoming very close friends. That is something which didn't seem so normal in northern Europe. There, work and private life seem to be kept separate.
>
> Australia is unusual as it has so many people from different parts of parts of the world that it's difficult to generalize. In my opinion, Australia seems to be somewhere in the middle between Ecuador and Germany. Here people socialize with co-workers on special occasions like birthdays, but still not as often as in Ecuador.
>
> I think that knowing your colleagues on a personal level makes it possible to work better as a team and just makes the job more enjoyable. Small talk and socializing with your co-workers gives you the opportunity to get to understand them better, to know what's important to them.

What does Diego say about the separation of work and private life?	In Belgium and Germany …
	In Australia …
	In Ecuador …
Why does Diego think socializing with co-workers and bosses is a good idea?	

Unit 03 Exercise 14

You are going to talk to your partners about what you did last weekend. Partner A will start the conversation. In your culture it is normal to wait five seconds after someone else has finished speaking before you say something. Always do this before you speak.

Unit 07 Exercise 14

With your partner, decide which of the situations from **14 A** you are going to use in your role-play.

Phone or go to see your partner, who is the customer service agent for the company, in order to complain. Before you start, make notes on what you expect from the company.

Unit 02 Exercise 14

It's your regular informal departmental meeting and everyone is giving an update on the status of their projects. Your project is not going too well but you don't want to discuss all the problems so ask as many questions as you can about the other projects.

Unit 04 Exercise 6

Conversation 1   You ( ) are the receptionist. You sound very bored during the whole conversation.

	Receptionist	Yes.
	Visitor	…
	Receptionist	Who?
	Visitor	….
	Receptionist	Oh, I'm sure he's busy.
	Visitor	…
	Receptionist	Well … OK.

Conversation 2   You ( ) are the visitor. You are very impatient.

	Receptionist	…
	Visitor	*(you interrupt the receptionist after 'welcome to')* I know where I am, thank you.
	Receptionist	…
	Visitor	My appointment with Bella starts in exactly two minutes.
	Receptionist	…
	Visitor	Yes. Where is she?
	Receptionist	…
	Visitor	Just tell her Sam/Sarah's waiting for her.
	Receptionist	…

Unit 05 Exercise 13

Hello all

The poll results are in but we still have to make the final decision. We have a choice between 31.05. and 04.06. I suggest 31.05. – I'm going on holiday on June 6th so it would suit me better :) Please send an email to us all if you don't agree.

We also have to decide on the place. Dirk is OK with Bonn so I suggest Sushirama because you can book a table there. The others are more like snack bars. Petra has been and recommends it. And there are plenty of other dishes for non-sushi eaters.

Is that alright for everyone?

Best
Manya

Unit 02 Exercise 14

You are on your way to visit a business partner. You get into conversation with the person sitting next to you, who is also on a business trip. Find out more about what they do and where they work.

Unit 03 Exercise 14

You are going to talk to your partners about what you did last weekend. Partner A will start the conversation. In your culture, silence during a conversation shows that the atmosphere between the speakers is not very good. Don't let this happen. Start talking as soon as there is a pause.

Unit 06 Exercise 1

Picture 1 shows how people express their opinions. In the West, most people say what they think very freely and directly. It is easy for the listener to understand the message. In the East, people don't express their opinions directly. It may be difficult for the listener to understand what the speaker really means.

Yang Liu has lived in China, Germany and the United States.

Unit 08 Exercise 13

Russia

- In some locations, exhibitors have to pay a surcharge if they don't use the fair organizer's own booth construction company. Monitor the work of local companies.
- Also, if you don't use the official forwarding agent, there will be extra charges when moving freight in and out of the halls.
- Order stand cleaning services separately from the show management.
- Smoking is usually permitted so have ashtrays at the booth.
- It's a very good idea to hire an interpreter if you don't have a Russian speaker at the booth. Take the time to inform the interpreter about your products.
- You should have bilingual company literature, signs and business cards. To avoid import tax, these things can be printed locally.
- In-booth hospitality is expected. Provide lots of food and drink, but people don't drink as much vodka as stereotypes suggest.
- Senior staff should be at the booth for negotiations. Take time to socialize with potential customers.

Unit 06 Exercise 16

What the British say	What they really mean
By the way, I was wondering if you'd had a chance to do that report?	This is what I really wanted to talk about.
Please think about this again before you start.	Don't do it.
It's probably my fault.	It's your fault.

Unit 06 Exercise 17

In indirect cultures, people prefer not to say no directly, especially not to the boss. It is very unlikely that Mr Nguyen would tell his boss that he can't finish the report by Friday. *I'll do my best* is a common way of saying 'no' so he probably assumes she realizes that. This makes it very embarrassing for him when she asks him to come to the meeting. Again, his answer *Yes, but it might be difficult* is an indirect way of saying that it's impossible. When he tells her that it's his son's birthday on Saturday, he expects her to tell him that he doesn't need to come on Saturday. When she wishes him a lovely party, Mr Nguyen thinks she has accepted his excuse for not coming to the office on Saturday.

Unit 08 Exercise 13

China

- Trade fairs are a vital sales and marketing tool in China.
- Chinese booth building companies are quite cheap, they know the location and what visitors like, but it's necessary to monitor them to be sure of quality.
- Use the official forwarding agent to avoid problems and delays at customs.
- All electrical work must be done by the official contractor.
- The exhibition halls are non-smoking but there is always a smoking area. Good idea to have ashtrays at the stand.
- It's a good idea to have Chinese staff at the booth for communication, but hiring an interpreter is also a must.
- It's a very good idea to have all important company literature translated into Chinese. Have it printed locally. Bilingual business cards are a must.
- In-booth hospitality is only common in large exhibits with enough space.
- Conservative, standard business dress is the norm.
- Don't expect immediate deals and signed contracts, or even negotiations on price.
- A Chinese trade fair is for information gathering and making contacts for future business so socialize with potential customers outside the exhibition hall.

Unit 03 Exercise 14

You are going to talk to your partners about what you did last weekend. Partner A will start the conversation. In your culture, it is important that everyone takes part in a conversation. If someone in the group is very quiet, encourage him/her to take part by asking questions directly like *What did you do?*, *What do you think?*

Unit 06 Exercise 1

Picture 2 shows how people deal with problems. In the West, if people notice a problem, they think the best way to solve it is to discuss it so that everyone understands that something is wrong. In the East, people prefer to avoid talking directly about problems. They don't think it is necessary as they are sure that everyone knows there is a problem and will find a solution without a discussion.

Yang Liu has lived in China, Germany and the United States.

Unit 07 Exercise 12

1   You could make a bad situation worse if you tell a customer that he/she is wrong.
2   You could say: *I'm sorry this is taking a bit longer than expected.*
3   This suggests you don't know what the answer is. Customers expect agents to have an answer.
4   You could say: *I'm sorry but I can't help you with that. Let me connect you to the department which deals with that.*
5   You have to apologize and show that you are working on a solution.

Unit 08 Exercise 13

Brazil

- In Brazil, your clothes show your status, so dress well.
- Taxation is complicated in Brazil so specialist help is a good idea. There are often problems at customs so it is better to rent a booth or hire a local stand construction company, but make the work schedules and deadlines very clear. 70% of construction workers building international exhibitors' booths must be Brazilian.
- Most fair locations have no air-conditioning so the exhibitor should have fans at the booth.
- It's essential to use an experienced forwarding agent. Official ones are best.
- Smoking is usually permitted in exhibition halls so have ashtrays at the booth.
- An interpreter is a must. Translate important company materials and business cards into Portuguese.
- In-booth hospitality is expected – also with alcoholic drinks.
- Order stand cleaning services separately from the fair organizers. Hire security services because many fairs don't provide this after the show closes.
- Allow time to talk to visitors. Brazilians like to do business with people they know.

Unit 04 Exercise 6

Conversation 1 You ( ) are the visitor. You sound polite and friendly.

	Receptionist	...
	Visitor	Good morning, my name is Mia/Mark Lee. I am here to see Mr Young.
	Receptionist	...
	Visitor	Mr Young. Nick Young from the purchasing department.
	Receptionist	...
	Visitor	*(getting a bit angry)* Could you let him know I'm here, please? I do have an appointment with him, you know.
	Receptionist	...

Conversation 2 You ( ) are the receptionist. You sound very professional.

	Receptionist	Good morning. Welcome to ... *(visitor interrupts you)*
	Visitor	...
	Receptionist	Of course. Who would you like to see?
	Visitor	...
	Receptionist	Is that Dr Menzel from R&D?
	Visitor	...
	Receptionist	I'll call her now. She'll be down in a moment, I'm sure. Who may I say is here?
	Visitor	...
	Receptionist	Please take a seat, while I tell her you're here.

Unit 08 Exercise 13

United Arab Emirates

- English is widely spoken so interpreters are not necessary. It is not a must to translate company literature, signs and business cards into Arabic, but it shows respect if you do.

- There may not be air-conditioning in the exhibition halls so make sure there are fans at the stands.

- Smoking is not allowed in the halls, but there will be a smoking area.

- There are no official on-site workers so you should hire your own to build your booth. There are no labour unions so you can choose a company to work with. Work crews may not speak English so make sure that there is someone who can communicate with them. They could be from India, Bangladesh, Malaysia, etc.

- It is a good idea to use the official forwarding agent.

- In-booth hospitality is only common in larger exhibits. Alcohol is not permitted.

- Men and women should be conservatively dressed.

- First meetings will be at the booth, but plan to arrange further meetings outside the fair grounds to get to know people better. This is a necessary step before doing business. Senior staff should be available.

Unit 07 Exercise 12

1　You could say: *I don't think that's completely correct.*
2　A customer may feel a bit sorry for you, but they want to speak to someone who knows what they are doing so won't want to hear this.
3　You could say: *That's a very good question. Let me just check that for you.*
4　It may be true, but the customer wants to get an answer.
5　You could say: *I'm sorry that you're not happy. I'll do my best to find a solution.*

Unit 07 Exercise 14

With your partner, decide which of the situations from **14 A** you are going to use in your role-play.

You are a customer service agent. Before you start, decide on your company's policy for dealing with complaints.

Unit 08 Exercise 10

You are the head of the stand construction team. You have finished all the work according to the instructions you got from the company and the team is getting ready to leave for the evening. There is one problem which your team only noticed this afternoon. The water connection to the stand is in the wrong place so there is no water at the sink in the hospitality area. The events manager of the company has just arrived and wants to speak to you.

Unit 08 Exercise 13

USA

- Trade shows in the United States are usually shorter than in other parts of the world – 3 days is typical. The main purpose is to give information and demonstrate products. Not many actual sales take place.

- To turn interest in your products into sales, you need a US sales office or an agent before you exhibit at a show.

- At most US trade fairs, only labour union workers are allowed to work in exhibition halls and move freight in and out of the halls. This results in higher costs than in most other countries so it is a good idea to contact the organizers to get information on the restrictions and costs.

- US shows use matchmaking technology to bring attendees and exhibitors together so it is necessary to understand how these systems work.

- International exhibitors who need a visa should be sure to apply early because the process may take several months.

- Customs regulations for importing goods to the US are complex so it is a good idea to use the official forwarding agent.

- All technical documentation should use the Imperial system of weights and measures (inches, feet, pounds, etc.).

- In-booth hospitality is not as common as in many other countries. It might even not be permitted. Only the most valued customers are invited to business lunches or dinners.

- Exhibition halls are always no smoking zones.

Transcripts

Exercise 1, Track 2

When you start a new job, you'll have a lot to think about, but do your best to make a good impression on your new co-workers from day one. Here are my five golden rules.

Number one is to make sure you arrive at work on time. This is essential. It's a good idea to test the route – by train or by car – during rush hour, so you know how long the journey really takes – and then add ten minutes.

Try to remember how people in the company were dressed when you went for your interview. You want to create the right impression by wearing the right clothes.

You have a lot to learn about your new job and your new company so don't be afraid to ask questions. Show the people you meet that you're interested in them and what they're telling you by making a note of the information they give you. An easy way to impress your new colleagues is by remembering the names and positions in the company of key people.

No one expects you to know everything about the company on your first day, but you can be sure that you'll impress everyone by knowing the latest company news. Set up an email alert to get news about your new employer and the industry in general.

If you don't know where people eat lunch, it's not a bad idea to take some sandwiches with you so you can eat with your co-workers in the break room. But if a colleague invites you to join them for lunch in the canteen or a café, just leave your sandwiches in your bag …

Exercise 7, Track 3

1   We're responsible for developing innovative new products.
2   Most of the suppliers we deal with are in Asia.
3   I'm in charge of the transportation of goods to our customers.
4   I'm familiar with international accounting standards.
5   Our department focuses on controlling the quality of our products.
6   I have a lot of experience of organizing orientation programmes for new staff.

Exercise 8, Track 4

1   I check the training needs of our staff and contact organizations which offer suitable courses.
2   I help to maintain our company network and deal with any staff computer problems.
3   In my department we focus on developing a market for our products.
4   We prepare reports on all the money that comes in and goes out of the company.
5   I'm responsible for making sure our products are made to the highest standards.

Exercise 13, Track 5

1   You're all so busy. Let me do that. I can stay late this evening. No problem, really.
2   Is that your little girl? Very cute. How old is she?
3   I saw you at the bus stop this morning. Shall I pick you up tomorrow morning?
4   Are you free next Thursday? Would you like to come over to my place for a drink?
5   Wow, it's lunchtime already! May I join you?

Exercise 16, Track 6

Please come back later. I have an appointment with my brother in a few minutes and need to check these documents beforehand. You know he's our chief financial officer. Maybe Stephanie's in the office. Why don't you call her?

Exercise 19, Track 7

Hi, my name's Qing. Many companies in China don't have orientation programmes, but my company is one of the strongest firms in China so we have a well-organized orientation for new employees. They join a training camp for one to two months. There they get an introduction to the structure of the organization, but the main purpose is to learn the necessary working skills. At the end of this, there's a competition and an examination. The American company I worked for also sends new employees to a training centre for around four weeks. Although it seems similar, in reality there are many differences.

The American company really wants newcomers to accept its culture from deep inside and feel part of it. They use games, parties, competitions and songs – just anything to get their message across. That's different in China because we have a kind of "boss culture". When a new boss arrives, the culture may change.

In the American company we learned a lot about working processes and, in general, we learned how to learn. Here in China, flexibility is more important so the company teaches us all the skills we need to be flexible.

Exercise 22, Track 8

Speaker 1

As a working mother – and I can speak for all the working mums in my company – I take a very short lunch break. Maybe about 15 minutes. We just eat a salad or a sandwich in the canteen because it's quick and then go back to our desks. We don't sit and talk to each other much because we want to save time. The younger people in the company – it's a Belgian law firm in Brussels, by the way – they tend to take longer lunch breaks and go out for lunch somewhere. The official language in our company is French although many of us are Dutch speakers.

Speaker 2

The local staff must take a lunch break from one to two o'clock. We even have to clock in and out. I work at one of the institutions of the European Union in Brussels, and by local staff I mean everyone who is not a diplomat. There are thirty of us so-called locals but in fact we come from eleven different countries. There are three official languages but you hear people speaking many different ones. Most of us bring a packed lunch and eat it in the canteen or at our desks. We do this because it is cheaper than going out. And if we have time, we go for a walk or go shopping or just stay in the office and have a chat.

Speaker 3

I work with a very international team of music researchers. We come from nine different countries and speak English to each other most of the time, but you often hear people speaking Dutch or Portuguese and sometimes German. Our institute is in Ghent. We only meet every two months so we always eat together in our lunchroom. A local sandwich bar delivers a selection of typical Belgian sandwiches because we simply don't have time to go out to get them. We don't meet very often so we want to make the most of our meetings. Everyone wants to be first in the lunchroom to choose the sandwiches they like best!

Unit 2

Exercise 1, Track 9

Speaker 1

At Messe Schweiz, we organize trade fairs in several locations in Switzerland. We welcome about 20,000 companies and over 2.3 million visitors to our exhibitions every year. Companies are often repeat customers, meaning we develop good working relationships with them.

Speaker 2

At the Malheur brewery, we use traditional methods to produce specialist beers for the Belgian market and for export. We specialize in dark beers, for which we have won prizes.

Speaker 3

At Metallbau Windeck, we manufacture high-quality metal doors, windows and facades. We offer complete solutions from planning to construction. We give expert advice and design our doors and windows to suit our customers' needs.

Speaker 4

At Canada Wood, we promote the use of products made from Canadian wood. To do this, we offer training courses to help designers and builders, and provide support for construction projects.

Exercise 7, Track 10

Agnes

When I came back to Kenya, I started working as a research scientist at a government institute. This has been a big change for me because I worked in the private sector in Germany and Switzerland before, where I often did overtime and sometimes even worked at the weekend. Now I always work the same hours, five days a week. This is nice, but I sometimes miss the flexible working hours I had in Europe.

Andreas

I work in Lyon, in the call centre of a non-profit-making organization which provides services to drivers in an emergency. Of course we have to provide the service round the clock and every day of the year. This means that I work shifts, including night and weekend shifts. We clock in and out because people start and finish work at different times. We are very busy during holiday periods so I often do overtime then, but generally I work a 35-hour week and have 31 days holiday a year including public holidays.

Lukáš

I work for a computer games company, but I've also just started my own company called Ice Factory. We started just over a year ago in Pilsen and I haven't had a real holiday since. I can't even tell you how many hours I work in a week because it depends on the number of orders we have. Our customers are mainly bars, clubs and hotels – places like that which are open in the evening or at the weekend. As it's a new start-up, it's important to be there for my customers whenever they need me, so that often means long hours!

Sandra

Metallbau Windeck is a family-run metalworking company. We have 120 employees so we are an SME. In general, our working hours are from 7 am to 3.30 but a lot of our manufacturing work is seasonal. This means that everyone does a lot of overtime in the spring and summer. All these extra hours are recorded in a working time account so that we can work less in the winter months to balance out the hours. For example, we usually finish work at 11 am on Fridays in the winter. No one has a problem with that!

Exercise 9, Track 11

My company has contracts with a group of European automobile clubs to provide roadside help for their members if they have a breakdown in France. I work with German customers mainly but sometimes deal with British or French customers, too. In our team we speak eleven different languages, but the most important ones are French, of course, English, German and Dutch. As far as possible, we use the language the customer prefers.

Our work involves taking telephone calls, text messages and emails from our customers and contacting the services they need. It's our job to send breakdown patrols to repair or pick up a stranded car. Then, depending on the situation, we co-ordinate everything for our customers. For example, we book hotels and rental cars for them and also help them to contact a doctor if necessary. We also help customers to keep in contact with the garage which is repairing their car.

As you can guess, for us the busiest times are in the holiday period. During that time, I deal with 75 customers a day on average. I'm a team leader so my role is also to train my team and check their progress.

As I said, our service is mainly for automobile club members, but we are also under contract to some car insurance companies and car manufacturers to offer this service to their own customers.

Exercise 16, Track 12

I'm a textile engineer, but when I talk to colleagues with non-technical backgrounds about my work, I try to explain things in a way they can understand. In Kenya, because so many different languages are spoken,

English is used a lot in business and I communicate with people who speak English at many different levels, from native-speaker level to a pretty basic level. This means that I don't only think about the technical words I use, but also check that I'm getting my message across. Sometimes, I have to repeat what I've said in different words, use simpler grammar, check that people have understood – things like that. And, of course, if I am speaking to foreigners, I'm careful not to use phrases that are only used locally!

Exercise 18 A, Track 13

I'm very pleased to welcome you here today, and glad that you are interested in getting to know our company. My name is Martin and I'm a senior manager at Penta-Electric. Let me start by giving you some background on the company. Starting in 1993 with a staff of 53 in the office in Switzerland, we now employ 138 people and have sites in Switzerland and Germany. We specialize in the automation of industrial processes for a variety of different industries and have a very large customer base in the chemical, pharmaceutical and paper industries. I understand that you want to hear about my department, so let me tell you a bit more about my role in the company.

Exercise 18 B, Track 14

I'm the head of the software division at Penta-Electric, where we develop software for industrial control systems for clients in a variety of industries. Basically, it's my job to organize the running of the department so that means managing staff and supervising projects. Among other things, I'm also responsible for calculating project costs.

My job also involves contact with our customers. I deal with all aspects of customer service and this requires a mixture of technical know-how, communication skills and commercial understanding. In our field of business, it's not enough to play the role of a salesman, we have to understand the technical issues our customers are dealing with. It's very important to develop a good personal relationship with customers in order to solve any problems. I'm lucky to have such an interesting and varied job, but it's certainly very challenging.

Exercise 22, Track 15

I work in technical support in the Frankfurt office of a big international software company. Because we are a global company, we provide technical support to our customers around the clock. For me, this means that I have to work eight-hour shifts, and this can be early, late or at the weekend. Because we all work at different times, we have to clock in and out. I usually work a 40-hour week, but I sometimes have to do overtime.

This was the same in my job in Vietnam, but there I only got 12 days annual leave. My work offers me interesting challenges because some of our clients' problems aren't easy to solve. I work with business clients, like banks for example, and you can imagine that if they have problems with their computer systems, we have to solve them very fast. Time is money!

Our customers could be anywhere in the world, but each of us specializes in certain markets because of the languages we speak. In fact, most of my work is done in German, but during the night shift, I sometimes work with clients in Vietnam because it's already the morning there.

Unit 3

Exercise 5 B, Track 16

1
A By the way, my name is Camila Machado.
B Nice to meet you, Camila. I'm Stephen Williams, but please call me Steve.

2
C Can I get you a cup of coffee?
D Yes, please, that would be great.

3
E Did you have a good weekend?
F Yes, thanks, very relaxing. How about you?

4
G I believe we met at the conference last year.
H Yes, that's right. I remember now.

5
I Beautiful day, isn't it?
J Yes, it is. Let's hope the weather stays like this.

Exercise 5D, Track 17

1

A Can I get you a cup of coffee?
B Yes, please, that would be great.
A Here you are.
B Thanks. This is just what I need.
A I know how you feel!
B So how long have you worked here?
A For nearly ten years.
B Ten years! That's a long time. Well, it must be a good company to work for.
A It is. I'm very happy here. What's your impression so far?
B Very good, but it's only my first week, you know.
A Of course.
B So, how many people work here? Do you know?
A About 120, I think.
B 120 – I didn't know it was so big.

2

A Did you have a good weekend?
B Yes, thanks, very relaxing. How about you?
A Oh, not too bad, thanks. I flew to Paris to visit a friend.
B Paris? Hm, that sounds good. Have you been before?
A Yes, for our first project meeting. Don't you remember?
B You're right, but I couldn't go for some reason.
A Well, anyway, it's a great place and I'm very happy my friend has moved there!
B I can believe that!

Exercise 7, Track 18

Diego	Hello, you're Carla, aren't you?
Carla	Oh, hello.
Diego	We met at the meeting this morning. I'm Diego.
Carla	Diego, yes I remember. Nice to see you again.
Diego	I'm just going to the canteen to get a coffee. Come with me and I'll show you where it is.
Carla	Great!
Carla	So how long have you worked here?
Diego	For nearly two years now. It's a great place to work.
Carla	I'm looking forward to it. My job is to coordinate a project with a new Italian partner.
Diego	Really? So I suppose you're Italian?
Carla	That's right. Originally, I'm from Pisa, but I've lived in Australia for over five years now. How about you?
Diego	Well, I come from Quito originally, but I moved here two years ago, to start this job, in fact.
Carla	Excellent! Adelaide's a great place to live. I love living here.
Diego	Absolutely! Me, too. So what did you do before?
Carla	I worked for a business consultancy – just a small company, but it gave me the chance to learn a lot.
Diego	Definitely. Oh, I'm really sorry but I've got to go, I've got another meeting. But it was good to talk. See you later!
Carla	Of course. Thanks for the coffee!

Exercise 18, Track 19

Our company's entertainment committee meets about five or six times a year.

There are five members of staff from different departments on the committee, plus one of the bosses to keep an eye on us.

The money for most events comes from a budget provided by the bosses. Events like the heart charity fundraiser are paid for by the staff. They buy cakes, tea and coffee, things like that. We have an event every year to raise money for a charity.

Our office quiz is just like a pub quiz, but in a private members' club. Two of our bosses are members so that means we can use it from time to time. We generally have some good prizes, such as a nice bottle of wine for each of the top three teams.

Our office quizzes are popular but, as you can see, there are more "wine downs" than anything else. There are a few reasons for that, I suppose. A "wine down" is easy to organize as it takes place in the office and it's only a matter of getting in the drinks – wine, of course, but also beer and soft drinks, and a few nibbles like crisps and nuts. There's no real food at these events. We have one every two or three months. We try to link each one to something that's going on at the time, such as Easter or Wimbledon.

It's difficult to think of events that interest everyone, but we try our best. Staff can choose to come to the events or not, but our bosses certainly expect everyone to come to the office dinner before Christmas.

Exercise 20, Track 20

Martin	Hi, Jakub, great to see you. I was looking for you all morning. There's someone I'd like you to meet.
Jakub	Oh, hello, Martin. I only arrived a few minutes ago. I missed the first presentation. I'm sure it was good. But who do you want me to meet?
Martin	Come with me. It's Maria Lopez and she's over there. You remember I told you about her on the phone? She's the network administrator at our head office who wants to find a job at the Polish office.
Martin	Maria, this is Jakub Rogowski from the IT department of our office in Warsaw.
Maria	It's nice to meet you, Mr Rogowski.
Jakub	It's my pleasure. By the way, please call me Jakub. Martin tells me that you're interested in working at our office in Poland.
Maria	Yes, that's right.
Jakub	I suppose you have friends in Poland.
Maria	No, that's not the reason. I speak some Polish and I'd like to improve it. Do you speak a mix of Polish and English in the office?
Jakub	Yes, we do. What languages do you speak? It sounds like ...
Martin	Excuse me for interrupting, but I'll leave you two to get to know each other. I'm the next speaker so I have to get ready.
Jakub	No problem. See you in a moment. I don't want to miss your talk, too.

Unit
4

Exercise 2, Track 21

F   I'd say that a safe environment is absolutely crucial. I mean, it would be too much of a risk to open a business in an area where there is a lot of crime.

M That's right, all companies want their employees to feel safe, but it's also the most important factor for the business premises. For me, good transport connections are just as important.

F   If you ask me, that depends on the kind of company. They are more important for companies which manufacture goods. I can't make up my mind about how important the local labour market is. If a company offers good jobs, they'll find staff.

M I'm not sure about that, to tell you the truth. I think a company should think about the potential for finding well-qualified staff in the area. What do you think is the least important?

F   I can't make my mind up about that either. Maybe the question of state funding?

M That could be crucial. I think a lot of companies need the financial support. I'd say that that is more important than some of the others.

Exercise 3, Track 22

Speaker 1

On my recent trip to Shanghai, everything went wrong. Because my plane arrived so late, there was no one to meet me. I wasn't sure whether I should just take a taxi or take the high-speed train.

Speaker 2

I came by car – and ferry, of course – from Rotterdam to London because I had a lot of samples with me. The company HQ is in the middle of central London and I just couldn't find the car park. It was hopeless.

Exercise 8, Track 23

I'm very lucky to work in such a beautiful environment, a lot more beautiful than in my previous company. That was just a normal office building. At my current company, it's our business to design and construct buildings made of wood of the highest quality so, of course, we work in one, too. When you walk up to the entrance, you see the wooden structure immediately.

The company headquarters in Shanghai consists of two buildings – our office and a show house. Our reception area on the first floor is huge. This is something typical of companies in China. In my old company we also had a big reception area, but this one is definitely more impressive.

Our client meeting rooms are also on this floor. We have a great view of the garden and the canal from here. Our meeting rooms are more comfortable than the ones in my old company.

Our kitchen is at the back of the building and the door next to the kitchen leads down into the garden. We often have our lunch out there when the weather is nice.

We have our offices on the second floor. We have an open-plan office for the technical staff and some of us have private offices, but we have an open-door policy. This is more Canadian style than typical Chinese. I share an office with one other person. Our top managers have their offices on this floor, too. In my old company, the general manager had a much bigger office. It's very common in Chinese companies for the boss to have a huge office!

Exercise 15, Track 24

Guide	I'm very pleased to welcome you to Metallbau Windeck today. I hope you had no problem getting here.
Visitor 1	No problem at all, thanks. The directions you sent us were excellent.
Guide	Glad to hear it. May I offer you something to drink before we start the tour? Coffee, tea?
Visitor 2	No, thanks. We're fine.
Guide	Well, let's just head down to the factory floor because there's a lot to see. I think I can promise you an interesting visit and show you just what you are looking for.
Visitor 1	What we've seen so far of your work has made a very good impression on us.

Exercise 16, Track 25

Guide	It's my pleasure to welcome you here today. If anyone would like to use the toilet before we start, they're over there.
Visitors 1 and 2	No, thanks.
Guide	So please just follow me down the stairs to the production area. By the way, please feel free to ask questions at any time. I hope you had no problems getting here.
Visitor 1	No problem at all, thanks.
Guide	Right. Well, as you can see, this is our production area with state-of-the-art machinery. I'd like to draw your attention to our new, highly innovative system …
Guide	Do you have any questions before we move on?
Visitor 2	Are the labs in this building?
Guide	Yes, they are. Just over there on the right, you can see our R&D labs. Before we go in, please put on this protective clothing.
Visitor 2	This looks very interesting. …
Guide	Well, that brings us to the end of our tour for today. I hope it has been worthwhile.
Visitors 1 and 2	Excellent. Most interesting.
Guide	So, if there are no further questions, let's head back upstairs. Some refreshments are waiting for us.

Exercise 21, Track 26

Hi Helen, this is Mark. I hope you hear this message in time because we've had to change the arrangements a bit. I've made an appointment for you with Mr Altmann for 2 o'clock tomorrow afternoon. His office is quite near your hotel, so it's not necessary for me to come with you. You can easily walk there, so please ask the staff at the reception desk to give you directions. I'll send you a text message so you can show them the address.

Let's meet at the bus station at 6 pm after you've seen Mr Altmann so that I can help you to get the shuttle bus to the airport.

Exercise 21, Track 27

Mark Hello Helen. Did you get my message?
Helen Hello Mark. Yes, I just listened to your message, but I'm afraid there's a problem. I've just left the Air China office. I couldn't answer your call because I was in the middle of making changes to my flight home. Something important has come up in Shanghai and I have to fly back a day early. I finally managed to get a flight tomorrow afternoon, so that means I can't meet Mr Altmann at 2 pm. Do you think you can …?

Unit 5

Exercise 5, Track 29

Working in HR, I generally communicate within the company. But there are times when, for example, I have a lot of recruitment to do, that I have to write or speak to people outside the company.

When that's the case, I use a mixture of email and phone calls. To invite someone to an interview, I'll first call them and then send a follow-up email confirming the details – time, place, etc. We sometimes have a telephone interview first and then always interview the people we're really interested in face-to-face, of course.

Once I know the result of an interview, I always phone the person to tell them the good or bad news. Direct contact is important for us here at Messe Basel. I would never send the result of an interview by text message, for example! That wouldn't fit our company culture.

As well as phone and email communication, I also have a lot of face-to-face contact too – partly in interviews but also in-house meetings.

If it's not possible to have a face-to-face meeting, because the people are too far away – we organize trade fairs in Miami and Hong Kong once a year – then I will have a video or phone conference. But I only have to do that a few times a year.

Otherwise, I mainly use email to communicate in-house. Everyone checks their email a lot, so I know that people will read them. Of course, if it's urgent, I make a phone call, sometimes landline, but usually mobile. We all have business mobile phones because the show grounds are so large and many people are not in their offices as much as I am.

Exercise 9, Track 30

Conversation 1

Katrin I'm phoning to tell you that your interview went very well. We were very impressed with your knowledge of the whole field of logistics.
Bella I'm happy to hear that. I've always enjoyed working in this area.
Katrin That's the impression we had, too. You'll get written confirmation of our job offer in the post by the end of the week.

Conversation 2

Pedro   Great to see you again, Katrin. How's the weather in Basel?

Katrin   A bit cloudy, but quite warm. Not as good as in Miami, I'm sure!

Pedro   You're probably right about that! Now, let's get started. Can you see the slides? I'd like to update you on how far we've got with our contracts for the temporary employees.

Katrin   Yes, I can see the slides, but I can't hear you very well.

Pedro   Is that better?

Conversation 3

Katrin   Everyone in the second group is very busy tomorrow so we'd like to postpone our lesson until Friday. Would that be possible?

Clark   Well, it depends on when we can meet. I'm in Lörrach on Friday morning, but I'll be back in Basel by around 4.30 pm.

Katrin   That sounds fine. I'll check with everyone and will let you know by this evening, OK?

Exercise 22, Track 31

Caller 1

Good morning Jan, this is Tomas. I'm calling about the list of special offers for our premium customers we spoke about yesterday. Could you email me the latest figures by tomorrow morning, please? Thanks.

Caller 2

Hello Jan, this is Julia Chen speaking. I'd like to have confirmation that you have changed the hotel booking for our delegation. Could you send it to me as soon as you hear this, please? We need it to apply for our visas. I'll call again later, at 3 pm your time because there are a few other things we should talk about. Speak soon.

Caller 3

Hi, Jan, Martin here. I'm ringing about the email you sent me yesterday. The date and time you suggest for a web meeting is OK with me. Do you already have an agenda? If so, could you send it by Tuesday morning? If you want to discuss the agenda first, just call me on my mobile. Thanks.

Exercise 2, Track 32

Maurício

In Brazil, senior executives have a very high status and they make the decisions. Of course, this also depends on the company culture and the personal attitude of the manager. Brazilians have a reputation for being very friendly and I think this is because everyone tries to act positively. This means that people try not to disagree openly so they are careful how they express their opinions and aim for a positive atmosphere. In general and in business, if there are problems, people "talk around" the issues.

Merlene

The Irish are well known for being talkative, and this is also true of people from Northern Ireland. People enjoy a conversation where people give their opinions freely on most topics, but an Irish partner will tell if you introduce a topic which crosses the line. If there's a problem, people will discuss it to find a solution but will always try to avoid conflict. In some companies, executives encourage employees to take an active part in the development of the business, but in others, the staff expect to follow instructions from the boss. It depends completely on the company culture.

Sarfaraz

In Pakistani corporate culture, the status of the boss is very high. The boss makes decisions and the employees expect the boss to do that. They don't expect the boss to ask for their opinion and they would not openly disagree with the boss whatever they really think. In general, it is not common in Pakistan to discuss things openly, especially if there are problems. In business, people wait and see what happens and only discuss major problems if it is absolutely necessary. There is a feeling that talking too much about a problem will make it worse and that a problem usually solves itself.

Exercise 5, Track 33

Victoria

People are often late for work in Argentina, so that some companies even offer bonuses to those who arrive on time. It is not so easy to be punctual because public transport is not very reliable and there is a lot of traffic on the roads. I'm always punctual for work so I'm usually the first person in the office! In general, meetings and appointments start more or less on time, but there is some flexibility. People in the company with high status often arrive late for appointments. If someone invites you for dinner at their home, you should never come on time because they won't be ready. 30 to 60 minutes later is quite normal.

George

In Kenya we don't plan to the minute, so if there's a meeting at 10 am, this means in the morning and not exactly at ten. However, people get to work more or less on time. The only real problem is that in the cities the traffic is so heavy so it's possible to be in a traffic jam for hours. This makes it very difficult to arrive anywhere on time if you come by car or bus, so no one is surprised if you are late. If you see that you will arrive very late, it's a good idea to give a call but it's not necessary to explain why. The most punctual people are the ones who can walk to work!

Hannu

In Finland, people think punctuality is very important in private life and in business. It shows respect to other people if you are punctual. In business it also means that you are efficient. This means that business meetings always start on time. If you are going to be even five minutes late, you should call to explain why and have a good reason. An Indian colleague once said to me that no one should be surprised if a meeting is scheduled to start at 9.17!

Kelsi

I come from China, but I'm working in India at the moment. I've noticed a huge difference in attitudes to punctuality at work. In China, being punctual is not so important in traditional culture, so in private life people don't worry about it so much. However, at work everything always starts on time; in fact, meetings may even start earlier than the arranged time so everyone will always try to be in the room a few minutes early.

In India, punctuality is not as important as flexibility and meetings often start much later than planned. For example, one of our clients invited us to a meeting at 10 am, but he didn't arrive until the afternoon and then told us that the meeting would be the next day. He didn't give us a reason as this is not unusual.

Exercise 7, Track 34

V Hello Gustavo, this is Vicky. How are you?

G Good, thanks. It's nice to hear from you. How's life in Stuttgart?

V Very busy as usual, but summer's coming so that makes life more fun. Remember that nice restaurant near the park we went to when you were here?

G Yeah, I remember.

V We had a working lunch there yesterday. That's why I'm calling. In fact, Peter Wegner asked me to arrange a web meeting for a project update.

G OK, that's a good idea because we have a few questions. The last meeting was very early in the morning here so would it be possible to find a time which is during our normal working hours this time?

V Sure, if we can find a good time. He asked me to suggest this Thursday. So, how about 3 pm here? That's 10 am with you, right?

G The time is perfect, but Friday would be better for us because we're meeting a client at 10 am on Thursday.

V Let me check our calendar. It looks OK, but I think Melanie is doing something on Friday afternoon. I'll ask her and then I'll send an email confirming the details. OK?

Exercise 10, Track 35

Our last project meeting was last Friday. It was a web meeting so we could share our desktops. This is more effective than a phone conference where we only talk. The meeting was for the software development team of our project. The team is based in Germany and in Brazil. Peter Wegner, our project leader, called the meeting for a project update. We're adapting standard HR software to meet the needs of our customers in Germany, Brazil and Italy. After a short introduction, Peter asked everyone to present the status of their work. So, we looked at the software for employee time management, payroll management and workforce management. We also discussed the arrangements for presenting the software to the final users in our clients' HR departments.

At the end of the meeting, Peter asked everyone to send certain documents and to fix dates for the presentations by the end of this week.

Exercise 15, Track 36

Peter	So, that's all for today. It's 4 pm here so it's time to finish. Gustavo and Ana, do you understand what to do next?
Gustavo	Yes.
Ana	Yes.
Peter	Good. I think we had a very productive meeting. Thank you and goodbye.

Exercise 25, Track 37

If a business partner from a country where people prefer indirect communication says *That's a very interesting point of view* it could be that he or she thinks what you've said is interesting. BUT it could also be a way of saying *I don't agree with you, you are totally wrong.*

I don't know a lot about this, but … probably means that the speaker is an expert and expects you to know and respect this.

Can we move on to the next topic? sounds very direct and almost rude if you haven't finished talking about the topic. In fact, this is a way of saying 'we don't want to talk about this anymore because we don't agree with you or because we can't make a decision ourselves'.

Unit 7

Exercise 2, Track 38

Ice Factory is a new company and it's still very small, but our client base is growing. Our customers can choose from a small selection of standard designs for ice sculptures, but our main business is creating special objects according to our clients' wishes.

We use clear ice of the highest quality and guarantee first-class workmanship. We offer our customers a wide variety of products – from glasses and bowls made of ice to complete table decorations, and from bars made of ice to installations created during live shows.

We don't get many orders from private customers – most of our work is B2B. Hotels, catering companies, bars, nightclubs and advertising agencies are our main customers. In our region, Ice Factory is the only one of its kind, so we don't have any direct competitors. The company is based in Pilsen and we don't work from any other locations yet. I think that will change because we provide an innovative way to create a very special experience.

Exercise 8, Track 39

Jeff	ASECCA Ltd. Jeff speaking. How can I help you?
Amy	Good morning, this is Amy Bishop from MC East. We're interested in recycling our e-waste, but we'd like to get a bit more information first.
Jeff	Sure. Let me tell you how the process works.
Amy	Great, yes.

Jeff	Well, the first step would be to set up an account. Then you would have your personal account manager here who manages the whole recycling process for you and answers any questions you have.
Amy	So, we would always deal with the same person?
Jeff	That's right. When you're ready to recycle some equipment, let us know and your account manager will contact you to find out what size kit you need. When the package is ready, an ASECCA driver picks up the equipment or we send a courier to collect it.
Amy	OK. Then what happens to it?
Jeff	We process the equipment and remove all your data from the devices. Guaranteed 100 %!
Amy	That's really important because we have a lot of employee information and client data on our PCs. Um, what do you mean exactly by processing the equipment?
Jeff	That's the recycling process.
Amy	OK, I see. And what happens then?
Jeff	Then your account manager contacts you to arrange for payment.
Amy	And we have the option to give the money – or part of it – to a charity, right?
Jeff	That's correct. When you set up an account, you'll get information on the details …

Exercise 16, Track 40

Speaker 1

I prefer appointments with customers in the morning. I love getting to know them personally.

Speaker 2

It was quite easy to arrange to meet later in the morning because she was doing something else at 9.

Speaker 3

Oh, I'm sorry. I must have forgotten to send you a written confirmation of the meeting with the people from the water sports company.

Speaker 4

We often get foreign visitors coming to the office. It depends on what I'm doing, but I try to spend a bit of time with them.

Exercise 22, Track 41

Let me give you some very interesting facts to show you how important it is to put more effort into improving customer service. Although using email or social media for customer service is much cheaper, it's not what customers want. A lot of people want to speak to an agent on the phone and, in fact, in the US, 92 % of customer service contacts take place on the phone. This is expensive for companies, but the worse thing is that 85 % of customers are dissatisfied with the service they get on the phone.

People give a lot of reasons for their dissatisfaction. For 72 %, it's because it takes too long to reach an agent. Nearly as many complain that they are put on hold for too long. But most customers get annoyed because it takes agents so long to find their customer information. 84 % said this.

I suppose that all companies realize that customer care is important for their business, but it is still a shock to find out that while satisfied customers tell around 5 people if they got good service, dissatisfied customers complain to 9 – 15 people.

Now, let me come to my favourite statistic – 89 % of dissatisfied customers stop doing business with the company and go to a competitor! That has to be a good enough reason to think about whether you are doing enough to keep your customers happy.

Exercise 1, Track 42

Maria   Hi, Steve, nice to see you. I expected to see you at the trade fair in Madrid last month, but I noticed that your company didn't take part.

Steve   Hi, Maria. You're right. Our management has decided to reduce the number of trade fairs we attend, and personally, I think it's a good decision. In general, attendance has fallen and customers can get all the product information they need online.

Maria   Yes, that's right, of course, but if you ask me, trade shows are still very important. I mean, you can never meet more people with a real interest in your company than at a trade show.

Steve   Could be, but these days we have to consider the cost of booth rental, all the services you need, hospitality for customers. It's a long list.

Maria   Well, I may be wrong, but I still think the cost per potential customer is still much lower than if you visit customers. I mean, we create all the promotional materials, company literature and things like that anyway. It's not only for an exhibition.

Steve   You're right, but there's also the cost of travel and accommodation for booth staff, and time lost at the office. As far as I know, our trade show results have never been that good.

Maria   Maybe, but customers are quick to think that a company is not doing well if they miss a fair. And there's no doubt that fairs are the best way to see what competitors are doing. I think you miss a lot by not attending.

Exercise 3, Track 43

Maria   So the purpose of the meeting today is to prepare for the trade fair in Basel so that Julia can start booking what we need. So let's look at the floor plan of the exhibition hall first. We only had an inline booth last time, but I think we should aim for something bigger this time.

Jan   I agree. I'd like to have something more open so that attendees have a view into the booth from all sides. To me, an island booth is worth the extra cost.

Julia   The island booths are generally in the areas of the hall which attract the most visitors. You know, near a hospitality area where people can get a cup of coffee. But they're always big. Look at this one – it's 28 square metres. That's very big – and very expensive. What do you think, Maria?

Maria   Of course, we'll have to check the budget to see if it's possible, but an island booth presents the company as one of the major players in the market so Jan's probably right that it's worth the extra cost.

Jan   Remember that we want to showcase the new dialysis machines, so we need space.

Julia   I'd just like to point out that up to now good booth layout has had a very positive impact on our trade show results.

Maria   So, do we all agree that the island booth we looked at is our first choice?

Julia   … we're going to offer in-booth hospitality, I suppose, so I'll order the catering equipment we need for the stand.

Jan   Can we move on to the technical equipment now?

Julia   Can we come back to that in a moment, Jan? I've got the stand cleaning options up on the screen at the moment. We need pre-event cleaning and the daily cleaning service, right? If we don't rent a standard booth but build our own, we have to order cleaning services separately …

Jan   If you ask me, we need to rent a fork-lift truck to move the equipment at the stand. Oh and before I forget, Julia, can you give us some information about the cost of the storage of empty containers during the fair? If we decide to buy the stand construction, we have to store it until …

Exercise 8, Track 44

The first step is to log on to our logistics tool and send a request for delivery. There is no charge for this. We process your request and then you receive a registration confirmation. Your delivery pass shows the date and exact time when your forwarding agent must be at the checkpoint in Basel. In Basel we have a very strict delivery schedule so the lorry must arrive on time.

Now you can commission your forwarding agent to transport your freight.

The next step is the arrival of your forwarding agent at the checkpoint with your cargo and delivery pass. Our staff there check the cargo and the documents. We have our own customs office on-site. After that the lorry can drive to the delivery zone.

At this point, our official forwarding agent unloads the cargo. There is a time limit of 30 minutes for unloading so this happens very fast. Then our agent transports the stand construction material to the booth in the exhibition hall and the exhibits go to the forwarder's warehouse. Finally, the forwarder transports the products to the booth the day before the fair starts.

Exercise 9, Track 45

Helpline agent	Good morning, how can I help you?
Julia	We have a delivery pass for 2 pm this afternoon at the checkpoint but I'm afraid we won't be there on time. Our forwarding agent has just contacted me to say that the driver is stuck in a traffic jam about 100 km away and it doesn't look good.
Helpline agent	Let me check your registration. … Yes, here it is.
Julia	What should I tell the driver to do?
Helpline agent	Tell the driver to continue to the checkpoint and go immediately to the counter for re-registration if he has really missed the reporting time. The counter is in the office building to the right of the entrance. Please tell the driver not to wait in line in the hope that our staff will let him through because that will only waste time.
Julia	Oh, no. Can't you give me a new delivery time now? That would save a lot of time.
Helpline agent	I'm sorry, but only staff at the checkpoint can do that. At the moment we don't know when the lorry will really get to the checkpoint. Please don't worry too much. If the lorry arrives before 4 pm, there's a good chance that it can be unloaded today. A lot of lorries are arriving late because of an accident on the motorway.
Julia	Oh well, thank you. I'll phone the driver immediately.

Exercise 16, Track 46

Speaker 1

As a Spanish speaker, I found the 'v' sound in English difficult, as it's normally pronounced like a 'b' in Spanish. So 'visit' sometimes sounded like 'bisit'. And I know that Spanish speakers often add an 'e' before words beginning with 's', like 'eschool'. I think we also sometimes get long and short vowels mixed up, so 'ship' and 'sheep' sound the same.

Speaker 2

My native language is Cantonese. When I first started learning English, it took a long time to get used to the vowel sounds, for example the difference between 'bat' and 'bet'. Cantonese speakers also find 'v' difficult – we try and say 'f' or 'w'. The worst though is 'th' – I really have to concentrate to avoid saying 'fee' when I mean 'three'.

Speaker 3

Like lots of other non-native English speakers, the 'th' sound is really hard. It doesn't exist in my language, Czech, and I still often get it wrong when I talk quickly. We also often get 'w' and 'v' mixed up – 'very well' might sound more like 'wery vell'.

Speaker 4

The stereotypical idea that German speakers say 'vell, vell, vell' is unfortunately partly right. We do often say 'v' instead of 'w' but I've mostly stopped doing that. In fact, when I know how a word is said, it's generally fairly easy. It's saying words I've only read which can be tricky – how can you know which version of 'ough' is right if you've never heard the word before! And I do sometimes slip up on the 'th' words – I 'sink' all too often. But, that said, it doesn't really seem to cause any problems, my colleagues – who come from various countries – generally understand what I'm saying.

Exercise 20, Track 47

Conversation 1

Meera Morning, Marcin. I'm sorry I'm a bit late.

Marcin That's OK. Gave me time to have a coffee. Let's go into the warehouse so you can show me which cases you need at the booth this afternoon.

Meera Great, thanks.

Marcin These are your cases here. So tell me, which ones do you need?

Meera Let me see ... Could you bring the cases marked J 108 to the stand? Do you think you could manage that by 2 pm?

Marcin Um, yes probably. I'll check with Daniel and send you a delivery note.

Meera Super. And while I'm here, we'll need those cases – M 206 on Thursday evening after closing time.

Marcin No problem.

Conversation 2

Meera Hello Marcus, this is Meera Kishore from Krishna Pearls. How are you?

Marcus OK, thanks. And with you? Have you sent a request for delivery yet?

Meera That's why I'm phoning actually. I checked the stand construction days and noticed that we only have two days to build the stand.

Marcus Yes, that's right. The 13th and 14th of March.

Meera Marcus, this year we have a very special display. We're very excited about it, in fact. I think you'll be very impressed!

Marcus That sounds very interesting. And from what you're saying, I think I know why you've phoned me!

Meera Well, I wanted to ask you if we could have access to the booth space a day earlier. Our construction team is worried that two days won't be enough.

Marcus Let me ask Stephan about that.

Video exercises

Film 1 – Presenting your company:
Malheur Brewery in Buggenhout, Belgium

Before you watch

1

A What do you expect to find out when someone presents their company? What topics do you usually mention when you present your own company?

B What do you think you will find out at a brewery presentation?

2

A Manu de Landtsheer, the CEO of Malheur Brewery, uses some special terms during his presentation. Put them into the correct category. Check the words in a bilingual dictionary if you're not sure.

blonde beer • bottle conditioning • bottle line • brut beer • candi sugar • dark beer • fermentation
hops • malt • yeast

ingredients	types of beer	beer-making process

B Match the definitions with three of the terms.

1 This beer is sometimes called champagne-style because of the way it is made.

_____

2 A part of the beer-making process called the third fermentation, which creates CO_2 naturally in the bottle.

_____

3 This is often used for making beer in Belgium. It increases the alcohol content and adds colour but, in spite of the name, it doesn't make the beer sweet.

_____

While you watch

3

A Read the statements and check any vocabulary you are not sure of. Watch the film and tick all the statements which are true based on what you see and hear in the film.

1 We are visiting one of the many small, independent breweries in Belgium. .... ☐

2 Manu de Landtsheer founded the brewery in the village of Buggenhout. .... ☐

3   Orange became the symbol of Malheur when Manu took over the brewery in 1996. .... ☐

4   Malheur is a microbrewery with a small workforce. .... ☐

5   There is a bottle line at the brewery, but not all the beer is bottled on-site. .... ☐

6   Malheur beer is bottle-conditioned and this means the taste improves with age. .... ☐

7   The brewery only exports to other European countries. .... ☐

8   The name of each beer is a number which shows the alcohol content. .... ☐

B Watch each sequence (as shown) separately and answer the questions.

1 (**00:00 – 00:50**)
  a When was the brewery founded?
  b Who owns it now?	

2 (**01:02 – 01:25**) When did the brewery get the name "Sun Brewery"?	

3 (**01:48 – 02:11**)
  a How many employees does Malheur have?
  b Which departments does Manu mention?	

4 (**02:12 – 02:20**) How much beer is produced per year?	
5 (**02:30 – 02:53**) What happens to the waste malt?	
6 (**02:54 – 03:18**) Which ingredients does Manu mention? a malt b barley c aroma hops d candi sugar e yeast f pale ale malt g spices	

7 (**03:50 – 04:10**)
  a Which countries does Malheur export to?
  b Do they have plans to expand their exporting operations?	

8 (**04:11 – 04:27**) How does the company ensure that their products are of high quality?	

9 (05:01 – 05:45)

What is special about Malheur 12?

10 (05:46 – 06:07)

What happens to the yeast in Malheur Brut beer?

C Choose the correct caption for each picture from the terms in **2A**.

D Choose five questions from **B** and adapt them to refer to your own company. How would you answer them?

After you watch

4 **A** Complete this short text about Malheur based on what you have learned about it in the film.

Malheur is a _____¹ company in _____². We produce _____³.

We ensure _____⁴ by using _____⁵. Our customers are _____⁶.

B Write a similar text about your own company's products or services.

5 **A** The film presents the company in these steps. Make notes on each section from memory.

- role of brewing in the Belgian economy
- location and type of company
- the history of the company
- the size of the company and its production capacity
- the production process: ingredients and production methods
- the customer base
- the products in detail

B Make notes about your company using the same structure.

Film 2 – Giving a company tour: Metallbau Windeck in Brandenburg, Germany

UNIT 4, PAGE 36

Before you watch

1

A What can you guess about the company from these photos?

B What pictures would give a good visual impression of what your company does?

2

A Oliver Windeck, the CEO of the company, takes us on a tour of the factory and explains what the workers are doing. Look at some of the technical terms he uses to do this. Put the words into the correct category. Check your dictionary if you are not sure.

> aluminium • aluminium profiles • to bend • CAD • CNC machine • to cut • doors • to drill • façades • frames • glass • high rack system • to sand down • steel • steel plates • to weld

activities • materials • finished products • semi-finished products • technology

B What activities would a visitor to your company see? Do you know the English words to describe what goes on in your company?

While you watch

3

A Read three descriptions of Metallbau Windeck. Watch the film and decide which is the best description. Underline any parts of the other descriptions which are incorrect or unknown to us.

> Metallbau Windeck is a family-owned company in the city centre of Brandenburg. When the Berlin Wall fell, it was a small company with 10 employees. Now it has over 50 employees. They are very busy all the year round. Most of the work is still done by hand by very well-trained experts. The company produces steel doors and windows for large construction projects in the area. They have plans to expand to a bigger site next year because they need to increase their capacity.

Metallbau Windeck is a metalworking company which specializes in steel and aluminium doors, windows and façades. It is located in a small business park a few miles away from the city of Brandenburg. When the Berlin Wall came down, it was a small company with 10 employees. The company has grown and now has a workforce of 120. Some of the staff work at the factory and others work on construction sites. Although some of the work is done by hand, it is a very modern factory which uses the latest technology for design and production.

Metallbau Windeck is a new company which was founded after the Berlin Wall came down. It moved from Brandenburg to Berlin in 1995. It produces steel and aluminium doors and windows for private customers. The factory is very modern and uses the latest technology for design and production. The workforce has grown very fast since the company opened. Most of the staff work on the construction sites so there are not so many workers in the assembly halls.

B Watch each sequence (as shown) separately and answer the questions.

1 (**00:38 – 00:57**) What does Oliver tell us about the history of the company?	His … bought the company for the price of … in … .
2 (**00:38 – 01:27**) What personal information do we find out about Oliver in the first part of the film?	
3 (**01:36 – 02:02**) He talks about what the company produces. Which of these does he mention? a aluminium doors b glass roofs c metal façades d large windows e skylights	
4 (**02:56 – 03:06**) Complete the description of Florian's work.	Florian … and sands … the frames of the …
5 (**03:29 – 03:45**) Hall 5 is the assembly hall. What happens there?	
6 (**04:09 – 04:39**) How does the company manage its inventory?	
7 (**04:50 – 05:06**) What is the job of the staff in the design office?	

C What would be the most interesting thing you could show a visitor to your company?

A Watch the film again from **02:29**. This is where the tour starts. Make notes on the information you hear.

B Write your own tour of the factory using all the information you have about the company. Play the film again from **02:29** without the sound and give the tour yourself.

C Apart from showing visitors different parts of your site, what extra information about your company would you include in a tour?

After you watch

5 Write five sentences comparing Metallbau Windeck with your own company. Use the expressions in the box to help you.

> Metallbau Windeck is …, but my company …
>
> … is (bigger) than …   … has more/fewer … than …   … is as … as …

6 Before the factory tour, Oliver shows us a model of the site and explains what happens in each building. Draw a plan of your company and label each building or floor. Use it to give an introduction to your company.

Film 3 – In my experience

UNIT 6, PAGE 51

Before you watch

1 **A** By 2020 about two billion people will already be using or learning to use English. Some are native speakers of English (inner circle), some use English as a second or official language (outer circle), and the largest group speak English as a foreign language (expanding circle). Put these counties into the correct category in the diagram.

> Brazil ● Canada ● India ● Italy ● Japan ● Kenya ● Northern Ireland ● Pakistan ● Poland

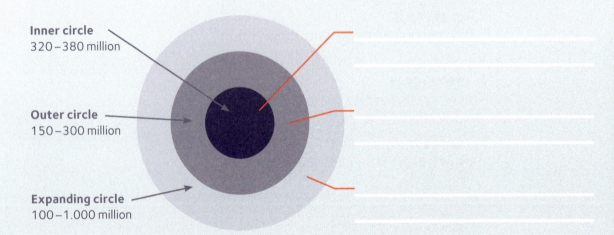

Inner circle
320 – 380 million

Outer circle
150 – 300 million

Expanding circle
100 – 1.000 million

B What does the fact that native speakers of English are the smallest group mean for the future of the English language?

C In your experience, is it easier to communicate with people from **a** the inner, **b** the outer or **c** the expanding circle? What are the reasons?

2

A In the film, three people talk about their experience of communication between bosses and staff. Match words and expressions from the film with an explanation of what they mean.

to flatter	a problem
to praise	to tell someone they have done good work
an issue	the way you do your job
a subordinate	to compliment someone because you want something in return
to monitor	someone who is lower than you in the company hierarchy
performance	to watch something or someone closely

B The main focus of the film is the way bosses give feedback to their staff. Before you watch, discuss these questions.

1 What is the purpose of feedback?
2 What different ways can managers use to give their staff feedback?
3 What makes feedback useful?

While you watch

3

A Match the people you met in the film with the circle they belong to.

Maurício   **Merlene**   **Sarfaraz**

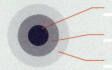

B Who is the easiest and the most difficult to understand? Why is that? Look back at your answer to **1C**. Do your answers match? If not, why not?

4

A Read the comments about communication between managers and staff. Based on what you find out in the film, decide which country or countries each one refers to.

Brazil	Germany	Northern Ireland	Pakistan	United States

a   It is very common for managers to praise their staff.
b   If a member of staff is not performing well, the manager usually calls a meeting of the whole team and talks about the problem in general terms.
c   If there are problems, managers don't criticize their staff's performance directly.
d   Bosses want staff to notice their own mistakes.
e   People give feedback, also negative feedback, very freely and directly.
f   Power distance is high. This means that staff show respect to the boss.
g   If a manager needs to give an employee negative feedback, the conversation will always start with some friendly small talk.
h   It is not easy to talk about one business culture. The relationship between boss and subordinate is different in different regions.

B Watch each sequence (as shown) separately and answer the questions.

1 (**01:00 – 01:24**) What difference has Sarfaraz noticed in the way staff address bosses in Pakistan and Germany?	In Pakistan, staff use … In Germany, staff use …
2 (**01:45 – 01:55**) What words does Merlene use to describe how people see the (Northern) Irish?	
3 (**02:20 – 02:26**) Merlene says that negative feedback is given *behind closed doors*. What does this mean?	
4 (**04:14 – 04:30**) What differences does Maurício mention between business culture in the North-East of Brazil and Sao Paulo/Rio de Janeiro?	In the North-East … In the economic centres …
5 (**04:47 – 05:02**) Why don't Brazilian bosses give praise for good work?	
6 (**05:05 – 05:13**) What are two reasons for giving feedback?	
7 (**05:40 – 06:40**) Sarfaraz explains how bosses and staff flatter each other. What examples does he give?	The boss says … The staff member says …
8 (**07:00 – 07:29**) Merlene talks about a *false comfort zone*. What does this mean? What example does she give?	

C What are the pros and cons of each way of giving feedback to staff?

5

A Read about some typical features of the English spoken in Brazil, Northern Ireland and Pakistan.

Brazil
Some features of pronunciation:
● well > [we*w*]   ● north > [no*rf*]   ● live > [l*eave*]

Northern Ireland
Some features of pronunciation:
● Good morning! > [G'd mornin']
● Ireland > [I*rr*eland]
Statements can sound like questions:
"See you later."
Like all native speakers, the Northern Irish use a lot of multi-word verbs.

Pakistan
Some features of pronunciation:
● where > [*v*er]   ● sport > [*i*sport]   ● hand > ['*a*nd]
Use of prepositions can be different from standard English:
"I was angry *on* him" (I was angry with him.) *The* and *a* are left out.

B Listen carefully to these sections of the film again and fill in the missing words.

Sarfaraz

(**00:54 – 00:56**) Power distance is Pakistan is quite _____ [1]

(**05:48 – 05:56**) I know you are _____ _____ [2] in performing

or managing people and tomorrow we _____ [3] some _____ [4] visiting.

(**06:37 – 06:45**) In this way, both the employer and the employee, they use such techniques leaving no _____ ⁵ for refusal.

Merlene

(**01:54 – 02:00**) But when it comes _____ ¹ problems or discussing problems, it would probably be the opposite. It would _____ ² very different.

(**02:10 – 02:16**) If you say _____ ³ or someone's not happy with you, you'll get some feedback on it.

(**02:36 – 02:40**) If it is serious, he'll then _____ ⁴, you know, call _____ ⁵ for an informal chat in your office.

Maurício

(**04:02 – 04:07**) We have _____ ¹ influences from different parts of the _____ ² in our country.

(**04:15 – 04:23**) For example in the _____ ³, we have – the behaviour is more _____ ⁴ and friendly and sort of _____ ⁵.

(**04:37 – 04:46**) Normally the bosses don't _____ ⁶ that much feedback so that in the end the staff does not really know if they are on the _____ ⁷ or not.

C Which features mentioned in **5A** do you notice? Do any of them make it difficult to understand the speakers?

After you watch

6 Look back at your answers to 2A. Were you answers correct based on what you heard in the film?

7 **A** In any discussion about methods of giving feedback, someone usually mentions the *Hamburger Method*. Match the descriptions with the pictures.

> In Japan, managers don't like to criticize an employee openly. Their strategy is to invite the employee who is not performing well to their office, but start and finish the conversation with positive feedback. The employee knows that something is wrong although the negative feedback is missing.
> In the USA, managers have usually learned to sandwich negative feedback between two pieces of positive feedback. They start and finish with praise for good work and in the middle of the conversation, they point out what has gone wrong. In Germany, people give their opinions directly so managers focus on problems and tell their employees what they think. There is no need to start and finish with positive comments if they only want to discuss the problems.

1   2   3

B Which method do you suppose managers in Brazil, Northern Ireland and Pakistan might prefer? Why do you think so?

C Which method would you prefer your boss to use and why?

Film 4 – Preparing for a trade fair: Messe Basel, Switzerland

UNIT 8, PAGE 68

Before you watch

 1

A In the film we see the preparations for Baselworld, the largest trade fair of its kind in the world. The film was made two weeks before the start of the exhibition. Match the words and pictures. Can you translate all of these words into your own language?

> booth • booth builder • box • building manager • construction • container • crate • delivery zone • elevator • exhibition hall • forklift operator • forklift truck • ladder • out of order • stand • stand construction materials

B What is happening in each photo?

C Have you ever been to a trade fair? Talk about your impressions.

A Read these quotes from the film. Think of the situation in the film and decide what the underlined parts mean.

1   This will be <u>a hotbed of activity</u> next week.
   a   The weather will be hot next week.
   b   The area will be very busy next week.

2   Tomorrow everything <u>will be shut down</u> for security reasons.
   a   The fair finishes tomorrow.
   b   The area will be closed to the public tomorrow.

3   Marcus is the <u>first point of contact</u> for exhibitors.
   a   Marcus manages the contact between the trade fair organizers and their clients.
   b   Marcus points out how exhibitors can contact the fair organizers.

4   This is where the boxes go up to <u>their final destinations</u> in the exhibition halls.
   a   The exhibitors can throw away the empty boxes here.
   b   This is the booth space rented by the exhibitor.

5   Daniel knows what to do <u>in an emergency</u>.
   a   He knows what to do if there is an unexpected problem.
   b   This is the place people go if they have an accident.

While you watch

In the film we meet some members of the Messe Basel staff. We see what happens during the preparations for a trade fair, but we don't see everything because there is so much going on. Find the six events which we see in the film and number them in the order in which we see them (1 – 6).

Stephan shows us stand construction work in one of the exhibition halls. .... ☐
A truck arrives late at the checkpoint. .... ☐
Workers unload containers in the delivery zone. .... ☐
Marcus welcomes us to the exhibition grounds. .... ☐
A truck arrives at the delivery zone. .... ☐
Zelal from Logistics speaks to one the exhibitors. .... ☐
Patrick connects the power supply to the stands. .... ☐
Daniel explains what happens if there's a problem with the elevators. .... ☐

Watch each sequence (as shown) separately and answer the questions.

1 (**00:18 – 00:30**) Preparations for Baselworld are in progress. What kind of fair is this?	
2 (**01:09 – 01:27**) Which department does Marcus work in?	

3 (**01:28 – 01:41**) What is the purpose of the visit?	
4 (**02:06 – 02:19**) Exhibitors at a fair can book different services. Which ones are mentioned? a catering equipment b cleaning c event planning d floodlights e internet connection	
5 (**02:20 – 03:00**) What happens after you send a request for delivery?	
6 (**03:00 – 03:24**) How long is the time slot for unloading in the delivery zone?	
7 (**03:50 – 04:01**) Why are the elevators so important?	
8 (**05:04 – 05:24**) a How many employees is Stephan in charge of? b What does his team do?	

5 Watch these sections of the film without the sound. Choose one and make up your own commentary. Make up any details you like.

| 1 **01:58 – 02:20** | 2 **02:22 – 02:58** | 3 **03:47 – 04:29** | 4 **04:36 – 05:00** |

After you watch

6 Look back at your answers to **2A**. After seeing the film, do you think you made the correct choices?

7 In his introduction, Marcus talks about the facilities and competences at the fair in Basel. From what you have seen in the film and have learned in the unit, make a list of what these facilities and competences are.

8 If there are videos on your company's website, choose one and describe what information it gives about your company and what its purpose is. If there are no videos, what aspect of your company's business would make a good film? Why?

Answer key – progress check

Unit 1 page 13

21

A Suggested answers
  1 You can make a good/positive/bad/negative impression on your boss/colleagues/co-workers by taking notes/asking questions/remembering key information about the company and the industry in general/arriving on time/being well dressed/turning up late.
  2 Why don't you invite your colleagues/co-workers/boss to your house/lunch/coffee?

B 1 of; 2 for; 3 with

C Suggested answer
  1 – Do you have any experience of chairing meetings?
    – It's my job to find out the needs of the company's employees.

  2 – Our boss has worked here for just under a month.   3 – Take some paper and a pen with you.
    – What is important for the satisfaction of our   – We deal with clients mainly from Europe.
      clients?   – I'm not very familiar with this new computer
    – I went for a client meeting last week.   program.

22

A speaker 1 C; speaker 2 C or A; speaker 3 B

B Suggested answer
Speaker 1 takes a short break, about 15 minutes, because she is a working mother and wants to save time. She eats in the canteen. She doesn't sit and talk to her colleagues.
Speaker 2 has one hour for her lunch break and she often has time to chat to her colleagues and even to go for a walk or go shopping. She doesn't go out to eat. She brings a packed lunch and eats it at her desk or in the canteen because it is cheaper.
Speaker 3 always eats together with her colleagues in the lunchroom because she only meets with her colleagues every two months and they do not want to waste time. They order sandwiches from a local sandwich bar to save time.

C 1 tend to take; 2 of us, at our; 3 for a walk; 4 most of the; 5 like best

23

A Suggested answers
  1 It's raining outside. Would you like a lift home?
  2 Are you free this Friday? Would you like to come over to my place for a drink?
  3 Wow, it's lunchtime already. Would you like to join me for lunch?

B 1 Thanks, that would be a great help.
  2 Great! That sounds like fun. / That's a nice idea. When do you want us to come?
  3 Yes, OK. Just a minute, I have to finish this email then we can go. / I'd love to, but I'm only taking a short break today.

Unit 2 page 21

20 1 do you enjoy; 2 spend; 3 am planning; 4 sounds; 5 involves; 6 makes; 7 do you deal; 8 are working; 9 am meeting

21 Suggested answers
1 As far as I know, the company was founded in 1949.
2 I'm pretty sure marketing is going to present their new sales strategy at tomorrow's meeting.
3 If I remember correctly, we employ 340 members of staff in total.
4 I may be wrong but I think we met at the last team building event.

22 1 F; 2 T; 3 T; 4 F; 5 T

23 **A** 1 on, for; 2 of, for; 3 in, about   **B** Students' own answers

Unit 3 page 29

20 1 Yes; 2 No; 3 They are at a conference.; 4 Maria and Jakub; 5 I suppose you have friends in Poland.; 6 He's the next speaker so he needs to go and get ready.

21 1 Nice to see; 2 I'm afraid; 3 How did it; 4 Not bad; 5 How was; 6 let's get; 7 15 minutes; 8 How has; 9 excuse me; 10 go ahead

22 **A** Suggested answers
1 anything; 2 been here; 3 see you again; 4 a good weekend; 5 your trip

B 1 c; 2 a; 3 b; 4 a; 5 b

Unit 4 page 37

25 1 most expensive; 2 much better; 3 a bit closer to; 4 more careful; 5 more impressive; 6 as good as

26 Students' own answers

27 **A** Asking for directions: What's the quickest way to the station? Where can I park my car?
At reception: Would you like to wait over there for her? What was the name again, please?
During a company tour: Have I answered all your questions? Shall we head back to my office?

B Suggested answers
1 Yes, thank you. Could I have a coffee, please?
2 The station is very close to our office. I would suggest walking.
3 The finance department is on the third floor. You can take the lift.

Unit 5 page 45

20 1 about; 2 for; 3 to; 4 of; 5 for/about; 6 on; 7 from; 8 on

21
1 I often take part in video conferences.
2 My boss is never late for departmental meetings.
3 From time to time we have meetings to discuss company strategy. / We have meetings from time to time to discuss company strategy. / We have meetings to discuss company strategy from time to time.
4 I am rarely away on business.
5 Every month I organize a project meeting. / I organize a project meeting every month.

22 Suggested answers
Caller 1: Tomas, wants latest figures from the list of special offers for our premium customers by tomorrow morning, please email
Caller 2: Julia Chen, send the confirmation of the changed hotel booking immediately, will call back
Caller 3: Martin, send the agenda for the web meeting or call to discuss the agenda first, please email/please call back (on mobile)

23 Students' own answers

Unit 6 page 53

23 Suggested answers
1 arrange/organize; 2 around/in/there; 3 works; 4 miss/rearrange/cancel; 5 rearrange

24 **A & B** Students' own answers

25 Students' own answers

26 1 When; 2 when; 3 if; 4 if; 5 when

Unit 7 page 61

21

A 1 D; 2 C; 3 E; 4 F; 5 A; 6 B

B Students' own answers

22

A *92 %* of customer service contacts are on the phone.
85 % are *dissatisfied* with this experience.
72 % of customers think it takes too long to *reach an agent*.
84 % of customers get *annoyed* because agents can't find their customer information.
Satisfied customers tell around 5 people about their experience.
Dissatisfied customers tell *9–15* people about their experience. 89 % of dissatisfied customers *stop doing business* with the company.

B Suggested answers
1 You should keep your customers happy and content.
2 You mustn't underestimate negative customer feedback.
3 You don't have to contact customers by phone.
4 You shouldn't annoy customers with dissatisfying service.
5 You have to keep customer contact details in a database so that the agent finds the relevant information quickly.

23

1 have to; 2 must; 3 don't have to; 4 had to

24

1 frustrated; 2 confused; 3 amusing; 4 challenging

Unit 8 page 69

19

1 dirty; 2 essential; 3 complex; 4 annoying, unexpected; 5 popular

20

A 1 a; 2 b; 3 b

B 1 You can tell that Meera knows Marcin better because their conversation is less formal: e. g. Greeting: "Morning Marcin." Vs. "Hello Marcus, this is Meera Kishore from Krishna Pearls. How are you?"
2 How Meera phrases her requests:
With Marcin: "Could you bring the cases marked J 108 to the stand? Do you think you could manage that by 2 pm? And while I'm here, we'll need those cases – M 206 on Thursday evening after closing time."
With Marcus: "That's why I'm phoning actually. I checked the stand construction days and noticed that we only have two days to build the stand." "Well, I wanted to ask you if we could have access to the booth space a day earlier."
3 Marcus is the more senior because Meera uses more formal language to speak to him.

21

1 I feel; 2 But don't you think; 3 I understand your point, but to me; 4 I agree;
5 In my experience; 6 that's just what I was thinking

Acknowledgements

Photos

Cover: Marco Baass, Berlin | **p. 5:** Shutterstock, lculig | **p. 6:** von links nach rechts: Shutterstock, tab62; Shutterstock, Phase4Studios; Shuttertsock, Minerva Studio | **p. 8:** oben: Fotolia, g-stockstudio; unten: Fotolia, auremar | **p. 9:** Angela Lloyd | **p. 10:** oben und unten: Angela Lloyd; mitte: Shutterstock, szefei | **p. 11:** oben: Fotolia, Brian Jackson; mitte: Shutterstock, Frank Fiedler | **p. 12:** beide: Angela Lloyd | **p. 13:** Shutterstock, MaraZe | **p. 14:** A, B, C: Quattro a/v group; D: Angela Lloyd | **p. 16:** von links nach rechts: Angela Lloyd; Shutterstock, racorn; Fotolia, goodluz; Quattro a/v group | **p. 17:** Shutterstock, Rob Bayer | **p. 19:** Angela Lloyd | **p. 20:** oben: Clark Stoppia; unten: Quattro a/v group | **p. 21:** Shutterstock, Dragon Images | **p. 22:** von links nach rechts: Shutterstock, Rob Marmion; Shutterstock, AVAVA; Fotolia, markos86; Shutterstock, v. s. anandhakrishna | **p. 23:** Fotolia, nyul | **p. 24:** Fotolia, bst2012 | **p. 28:** Shutterstock, Poznyakov | **p. 29:** Fotolia, WavebreakMediaMicro | **p. 30:** von links nach rechts: Fotolia, Velirina; Fotolia, Speedfighter; Fotolia, ArTo; Fotolia, Pavel Losevsky; Shutterstock, Sergey Kelin | **p. 31:** oben: Shutterstock, Stephen Rees; mitte von links nach rechts: Fotolia, nyul; Shutterstock, Monkey Business Images; Shutterstock, cristovao | **p. 32:** Angela Lloyd | **p. 34:** oben: Shutterstock, Mega Pixel; mitte: SOFAROBOTNIK GbR, Augsburg & München | **p. 35:** Fotolia, Robert Kneschke | **p. 36:** oben: Shutterstock, Odua Images; mitte: Shutterstock, Andre Jabali; unten: Quattro a/v group | **p. 41:** Quattro a/v group | **p. 44:** Cartoonstock, Roy Delgado | **p. 45:** Shutterstock, Andresr | **p. 46:** oben: Yang Liu Design, Berlin; unten: Quattro a/v group | **p. 47:** oben: Yang Liu Design, Berlin; unten: Shutterstock, Aaron Amat | **p. 48:** Angela Lloyd | **p. 49:** Shutterstock, Ldprod | **p. 50:** Shutterstock, Monkey Business Images | **p. 51:** Shutterstock, Dragon Images | **p. 53:** Shutterstock, StockLite | **p. 54:** oben: von links nach rechts: Shutterstock, Kekyalyaynen; Shutterstock, alterfalter; Shutterstock, nmedia; Shutterstock, Thor Jorgen Udvang; unten: Angela Lloyd | **p. 56:** Shutterstock, michaeljung | **p. 57:** Shutterstock, Ivelin Radkov | **p. 59:** Shutterstock; Lightspring | **p. 61:** Shutterstock, CREATISTA | **p. 62:** oben: Fotolia, Dmitriy Danilenko; unten: Shutterstock, Katarina Fox | **p. 65:** oben: Quattro a/v group; unten: Shutterstock, juniart | **p. 67:** Shutterstock, chevanon | **p. 68:** Quattro a/v group | **p. 69:** Quattro a/v group | **p. 97:** Quattro a/v group | **p. 98:** 1: picture alliance / ZB; 2, 5, 6: Angela Lloyd; 3, 4: Quattro a/v group | **p. 104:** Quattro a/v group

Illustrations

p. 7, 15, 25, 33, 40, 63, 103: Natascha Römer, RÖMER & OS ADTSCHIJ – Visualisierungen GbR, Schwäbisch Gmünd

Track list

Track	Exercise	Length
01	Copyright	00:10
Unit 01		
02	1	01:45
03	7	00:48
04	8	00:48
05	13	00:46
06	16 & 18	00:43
07	19	01:33
08	22	02:16
Unit 02		
09	1	01:19
10	7	02:37
11	9	01:37
12	16	00:55
13	18	00:52
14	18	01:06
15	22	01:26
Unit 03		
16	5B	00:52
17	5D	01:33
18	7	01:41
19	18	01:42
20	20	01:21
Unit 04		
21	2	01:12
22	3	00:40
23	8	01:52
24	15	00:41
25	16	01:17
26	21	00:45
27	21	00:37
28	22	00:17

Track	Exercise	Length
Unit 05		
29	5	02:07
30	9	01:42
31	22	01:10
Unit 06		
32	2	02:24
33	5	03:27
34	7	01:20
35	10	01:05
36	15	00:22
37	25	00:55
Unit 07		
38	2	01:26
39	8	01:40
40	16	00:47
41	22	01:38
Unit 08		
42	1	01:50
43	3	02:29
44	8	01:19
45	9	01:31
46	16	02:26
47	20	01:57

The Soundhouse, London
Direction: James Richardson
Sound engineer: Darrin Bowen
Speakers: James Goode, Dave John, Shaheen Khan, Klemens Koehring, Glen McCready, Eric Meyers, Debra Michaels, Kris Milnes, Juliet Prague, Natascha Slasten, Yolanda Vasquez, Qiang Wu, Chuanzi Xing